W9-AYH-844

Bethlehem
Area Public Library
1901 *Celebrating 100 years* 2001

BETHLEHEM, PENNSYLVANIA 18018

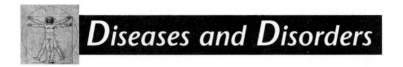
Diseases and Disorders

Diabetes

Diabetes

Titles in the Diseases and Disorders series include:

Alzheimer's Disease
Anorexia and Bulimia
Arthritis
Asthma
Attention Deficit Disorder
Autism
Breast Cancer
Chronic Fatigue Syndrome
Cystic Fibrosis
Down Syndrome
Epilepsy
Hemophilia
Hepatitis
Learning Disabilities
Leukemia
Lyme Disease
Multiple Sclerosis
Phobias
Schizophrenia
Sleep Disorders

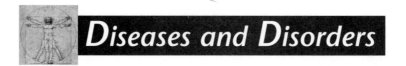

Diseases and Disorders

Diabetes

by Barbara Sheen

LUCENT
BOOKS®

THOMSON
———————✳———™
GALE

San Diego • Detroit • New York • San Francisco • Cleveland
New Haven, Conn. • Waterville, Maine • London • Munich

THOMSON

————✦————™

GALE

In Memory of my Father

© 2003 by Lucent Books. Lucent Books is an imprint of The Gale Group, Inc.,
a division of Thomson Learning, Inc.

Lucent Books® and Thomson Learning™ are trademarks used herein under license.

For more information, contact
Lucent Books
27500 Drake Rd.
Farmington Hills, MI 48331-3535
Or you can visit our Internet site at www.gale.com

ALL RIGHTS RESERVED.
No part of this work covered by the copyright hereon may be reproduced or used in any form or by any
means—graphic, electronic, or mechanical, including photocopying, recording, taping, Web distribution
or information storage retrieval systems—without the written permission of the publisher.

LIBRARY OF CONGRESS CATALOGING-IN-PUBLICATION DATA

Sheen, Barbara.
  Diabetes / by Barbara Sheen.
      v. cm.— (Diseases and disorders series)
Includes bibliographical references and index.
Summary: Describes how to diagnose and treat diabetes. Offers alternative
treatment and what the future holds for those living with diabetes.
  ISBN 1-59018-244-8
  1. Diabetes—Juvenile literature. [1. Diabetes. 2. Diseases.] I.Title. II. Series.
  RC660.5 .S53 2003
  616.4'62—dc21

                                                                          2002013620

Printed in the United States of America

Table of Contents

Foreword   8

Introduction:
  A Developing Epidemic   10

Chapter 1
  What Is Diabetes?   14

Chapter 2
  Diagnosis and Treatment   29

Chapter 3
  Alternative and Complementary Treatment   45

Chapter 4
  Living with Diabetes   62

Chapter 5
  What the Future Holds   78

  Notes   92
  Glossary   96
  Organizations to Contact   98
  For Further Reading   100
  Works Consulted   103
  Index   106
  Picture Credits   111
  About the Author   112

"The Most Difficult Puzzles Ever Devised"

CHARLES BEST, ONE of the pioneers in the search for a cure for diabetes, once explained what it is about medical research that intrigued him so. "It's not just the gratification of knowing one is helping people," he confided, "although that probably is a more heroic and selfless motivation. Those feelings may enter in, but truly, what I find best is the feeling of going toe to toe with nature, of trying to solve the most difficult puzzles ever devised. The answers are there somewhere, those keys that will solve the puzzle and make the patient well. But how will those keys be found?"

Since the dawn of civilization, nothing has so puzzled people—and often frightened them, as well—as the onset of illness in a body or mind that had seemed healthy before. A seizure, the inability of a heart to pump, the sudden deterioration of muscle tone in a small child—being unable to reverse such conditions or even to understand why they occur was unspeakably frustrating to healers. Even before there were names for such conditions, even before they were understood at all, each was a reminder of how complex the human body was, and how vulnerable.

While our grappling with understanding diseases has been frustrating at times, it has also provided some of humankind's most heroic accomplishments. Alexander Fleming's accidental discovery in 1928 of a mold that could be turned into penicillin has resulted in the saving of untold millions of lives. The isolation of the enzyme insulin has reversed what was once a death sentence for anyone with diabetes. There have been great strides in combating conditions for which there is not yet a cure, too. Medicines can help AIDS patients live longer, diagnostic tools such as mammography and ultrasounds can help doctors find tumors while they are treatable, and laser surgery techniques have made the most intricate, minute operations routine.

This "toe-to-toe" competition with diseases and disorders is even more remarkable when seen in a historical continuum. An astonishing amount of progress has been made in a very short time. Just two hundred years ago, the existence of germs as a cause of some diseases was unknown. In fact, it was less than 150 years ago that a British surgeon named Joseph Lister had difficulty persuading his fellow doctors that washing their hands before delivering a baby might increase the chances of a healthy delivery (especially if they had just attended to a diseased patient)!

Each book in Lucent's *Diseases and Disorders* series explores a disease or disorder and the knowledge that has been accumulated (or discarded) by doctors through the years. Each book also examines the tools used for pinpointing a diagnosis, as well as the various means that are used to treat or cure a disease. Finally, new ideas are presented—techniques or medicines that may be on the horizon.

Frustration and disappointment are still part of medicine, for not every disease or condition can be cured or prevented. But the limitations of knowledge are being pushed outward constantly; the "most difficult puzzles ever devised" are finding challengers every day.

A Developing Epidemic

CHELSEA WAS TWELVE when she was diagnosed with diabetes. She had been feeling weak and tired for quite some time. Then, right after her twelfth birthday, her symptoms worsened. She experienced extreme hunger and thirst, and had to urinate frequently. Chelsea explains: "I was drinking gallons of water every day, and I was eating more than my three older brothers combined. Even worse, I had to go to the bathroom constantly. I had to go after each of my classes every day, and sometimes I thought I would explode before the school bus reached my street."[1] When Chelsea's parents took her to the doctor, Chelsea found out that like millions of other people throughout the world, she had diabetes.

A Serious Disease

Diabetes is a disease that affects a person's ability to convert glucose, or sugar, to energy. It is a serious disease without a cure and can cause significant damage to every part of a person's body.

Currently, diabetes is the sixth leading cause of death in the United States. It affects one in every seven Americans, with more than twenty two hundred new cases diagnosed every day. And, these numbers are growing rapidly. Experts at the Centers for Disease Control and Prevention predict that by 2050 the number of Americans diagnosed with diabetes will increase by 165 percent. Therefore, health care experts are calling the rising incidence of diabetes a developing diabetes epidemic. They predict this epidemic will have a tremendous impact on the health of all Americans in the twenty-first century.

This problem is not limited to the United States. At the present time, 140 million people worldwide have diabetes, and this number is expected to double by 2025. Diabetes rates are especially troubling in Australia and Asia, where the incidence of diabetes is skyrocketing. For example, although Australia has a population of only about 19 million people, more than nine hundred thousand Australians have diabetes. And a new case of diabetes is being diagnosed every ten minutes in Australia.

The statistics are even more disconcerting in Asia where 60 million people have diabetes. That figure is expected to grow to at least 115 million people by 2025, making diabetes the fastest-growing disease in Asia. Clive Cockram of the Asia Pacific Policy Group warns: "The diabetes trend [in Asia] could be devastating."[2]

A woman with diabetes injects herself with the insulin her body needs to regulate the level of sugar in her bloodstream.

Problems for Individuals and Society

Making matters worse, more than one-third of all the people worldwide with diabetes do not know they have it. For this reason, many will not find out until they have developed life-threatening complications caused by the disease. This causes problems for afflicted individuals, their families, and society. Experts estimate that diabetes costs American society $98 billion per year in medical costs, disability payments, and lost income, an amount that far exceeds the yearly national income of many emerging nations. According to Dr. Jeff Koplan of the Centers for Disease Control and Prevention, "If these dangerous trends continue at

Regular exercise is part of these patients' diabetes management program.

the current rates, the impact on the nation's health and medical costs in the future will be overwhelming."[3]

Because the impact of diabetes is so far-reaching, it is important that people understand more about it. Therefore, government organizations throughout the world, including the U.S. National Institutes of Health, have instituted programs to raise public awareness of diabetes. These programs have a twofold purpose. They may be able to compel people who are unaware that they have diabetes to seek diagnosis, and encourage people without diabetes to take steps to help keep themselves from developing the disease. Moreover, by understanding what causes diabetes, how to best treat it, and the challenges it presents, friends and family members will understand more clearly how to provide diabetes sufferers with support and help. Patients and their families will be able to make better choices about their treatment and learn better ways to manage and control the disease. This type of knowledge should help to limit the devastating impact diabetes has on individuals and society.

Winning the Battle Against Diabetes

At seventeen, Chelsea has learned quite a bit about diabetes and how to manage it. "After I was diagnosed with diabetes,"she explains, "there was so much to learn. Not just for me, but for my whole family. Keeping diabetes under control really depends on so many things. You can't succeed unless you know what you're up against."[4]

So far, Chelsea has succeeded quite well. She is a busy and popular student. Like many other teenagers she attends high school, has an active social life, and looks forward to the future. She explains: "Having diabetes has changed a lot of things about my lifestyle, but it hasn't changed who I am or stopped me from living a normal life. I plan to go to college and major in biology. Then I plan to become a veterinarian. That's my dream."[5] With proper treatment, Chelsea, like millions of other people with diabetes, can live a normal and productive life, one in which her dream is quite likely to come true.

Chapter 1

What Is Diabetes?

Diabetes is a disease that interferes with the way the body uses food for growth and energy. When food is eaten it is broken down by the digestive system and converted to glucose, a form of simple sugar that gives the cells energy to perform their many functions. Glucose is the body's primary source of fuel. Without glucose, the body becomes weak and fatigued, and eventually starves.

After digestion, glucose is sent into the bloodstream where it travels to cells throughout the body to provide them with fuel. However because thin walls surround every cell, glucose cannot pass from the bloodstream into the cells without the help of a hormone, a type of chemical, called insulin.

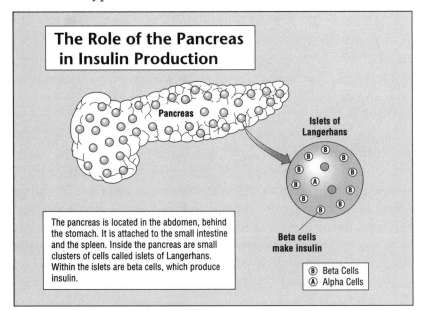

The Role of the Pancreas in Insulin Production

Pancreas

Islets of Langerhans

Beta cells make insulin

The pancreas is located in the abdomen, behind the stomach. It is attached to the small intestine and the spleen. Inside the pancreas are small clusters of cells called islets of Langerhans. Within the islets are beta cells, which produce insulin.

Ⓑ Beta Cells
Ⓐ Alpha Cells

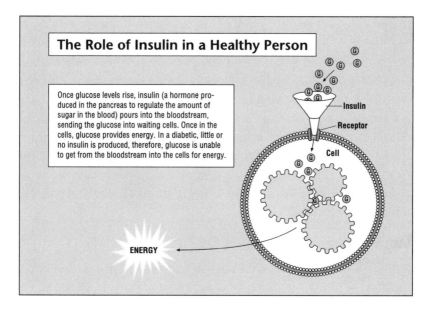

The Role of Insulin in a Healthy Person

Once glucose levels rise, insulin (a hormone produced in the pancreas to regulate the amount of
sugar in the blood) pours into the bloodstream,
sending the glucose into waiting cells. Once in the
cells, glucose provides energy. In a diabetic, little or
no insulin is produced, therefore, glucose is unable
to get from the bloodstream into the cells for energy.

Insulin

Receptor

Cell

ENERGY

Insulin acts like a key. It travels throughout the body, opening
the thin walls of the cells so that glucose can pass through. Insulin is produced in the pancreas, an organ located between the
stomach and the liver, whose main job is manufacturing insulin
and controlling the body's use of the hormone.

After glucose enters the cells, the cells immediately use glucose for energy. Or, if the glucose is not needed immediately,
cells in the liver convert it and store it in a form known as glycogen for later use.

Generally, after people eat, their glucose levels rise. As a result, the pancreas produces insulin so that the cells can absorb
and use glucose. Between meals, when there is no new food for
the digestive system to break down, blood glucose levels fall,
and the pancreas releases less insulin. When the body needs
more energy, glycogen is released into the bloodstream causing
insulin levels to rise once again. In this way, the pancreas main-
tains a balance between the level of sugar and the level of insulin
in the bloodstream. It makes sure insulin is available whenever
it is needed to help the cells absorb glucose.

When people have diabetes, this balance is not maintained.
People with diabetes produce insufficient insulin. Without insulin

to open the cell walls, the cells of people with diabetes do not get the fuel they need and become starved for energy. So, when diabetics digest food, glucose builds up to dangerous levels in their bloodstream. High levels of blood glucose can be toxic, causing problems throughout the body. For this reason, the body tries to get rid of excess glucose. The kidneys, whose job it is to rid the body of toxins, produce large quantities of urine in order to flush the excess glucose out of the body. However, when blood glucose levels are too high, the body cannot produce enough urine to eliminate the surplus glucose. Thus, abnormal levels of glucose remain in the blood.

What Type of Disease Is Diabetes?

No one knows exactly what causes diabetes or why some people develop it. However, diabetes is a chronic disease and once a person develops it there is no cure. When people have diabetes the symptoms may come and go, but the disease itself affects them for life. A diabetic talks about his reaction to learning he had a chronic disease: "I can still remember the day I was diagnosed with diabetes in September of 1961. It was the day I lost my innocence. My overwhelming thought at the time was what am I going to lose? Would I never be able to eat dessert again? Could I still play sports? Would I lose my eyesight? However . . . having lived with diabetes for the past thirty-six years, and having accepted it as my lifetime partner, I have dedicated my life to win the battle against diabetes!"[6]

In addition to being a chronic disease, in some cases diabetes is also an autoimmune disease. An autoimmune disease is a disease in which the immune system, which protects the body from foreign invaders like bacteria or viruses, mistakes cells in the body for foreign invaders and sends white blood cells to attack and destroy them. In diabetes, the immune system attacks and destroys beta cells, the cells in the pancreas that produce insulin. As a result, the pancreas cannot manufacture sufficient insulin to regulate blood glucose levels.

Scientists do not know why the immune system acts in this way. Some scientists hypothesize that exposure to an unknown virus triggers changes in the pancreas that cause the immune system to attack. Others believe that certain people have a genetic tendency to develop autoimmune diseases. No matter what the reason, the result is lack of insulin and high blood glucose.

Two Types of Diabetes

There are two main types of diabetes, type I and type II diabetes. Both are chronic diseases and both result in high levels of glucose in the bloodstream. However the reason this occurs, differs. Type I diabetes is an autoimmune disease in which the body loses its ability to produce insulin. As a result, people with type I diabetes must take daily insulin injections to stay alive.

Type I diabetes used to be known as juvenile onset diabetes. This is because type I diabetes most often strikes children and young adults. It often begins suddenly, and is the most severe type of diabetes. It affects about 1 million Americans, about 10 percent of all diabetics. A child with type I diabetes talks about his condition: "I was diagnosed with diabetes four days before my first birthday. I am 6 ½ now. I have been giving myself shots [without the help of his parents] since I was 5. It is just the way it is."[7]

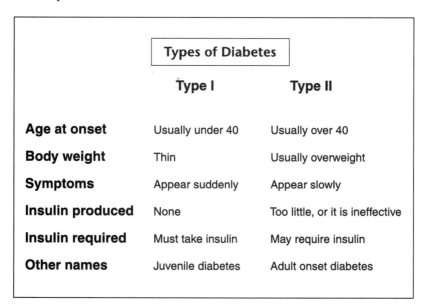

Types of Diabetes		
	Type I	**Type II**
Age at onset	Usually under 40	Usually over 40
Body weight	Thin	Usually overweight
Symptoms	Appear suddenly	Appear slowly
Insulin produced	None	Too little, or it is ineffective
Insulin required	Must take insulin	May require insulin
Other names	Juvenile diabetes	Adult onset diabetes

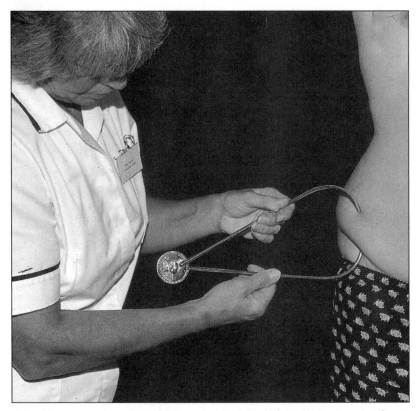

A health care worker uses calipers to measure body fat; obesity is a significant factor in the development of type II diabetes.

Type II diabetes, on the other hand, usually develops in people over forty and increases in frequency as people get older. It affects 16 million Americans. It generally begins gradually, and is less severe than type I diabetes. Type II diabetes is not an autoimmune disease. In type II diabetes, the pancreas produces insulin, but not enough to regulate blood glucose levels. And, the cells of people with type II diabetes do not respond to the insulin that is produced. Instead, the cells of people with type II diabetes resist insulin. This makes it impossible for glucose to enter the cells. According to diabetes expert, Dr. Alan L. Rubin, "Those with type 2 diabetes have insulin in their bodies, but their bodies respond to insulin in abnormal ways. Those with type 2 diabetes are insulin-resistant, meaning that their bodies resist the normal healthy functioning of insulin. This insulin resistance combined with not enough insulin causes type 2 diabetes."[8]

People at Risk

Although there is no way of predicting who will get diabetes and no way to prevent it, there are certain people who appear to be at greater risk. Among these are people who are overweight. Overweight people are more likely than thin people to develop type II diabetes. Research investigating the link between weight and the risk of developing diabetes has shown that nine out of ten people who are newly diagnosed with type II diabetes are overweight. In addition, the study found that the longer people have been overweight the more likely they are to develop diabetes. People who have been overweight for ten years or more are the most likely to get diabetes.

In a similar study the weight of a group of nurses was compared to the incidence of diabetes. This study found that the incidence of diabetes in the most overweight or obese nurses was more than one hundred times greater than in the thinner nurses. Even nurses who were only slightly overweight were three times more likely to have diabetes than their thinner peers were. Scientists are unsure why this occurs. However, they hypothesize that when people consistently overeat, the pancreas cannot manufacture enough insulin to regulate the large quantity of glucose that is produced.

The way body weight is distributed also appears to put people at risk. Most overweight people who develop diabetes carry a large part of their weight around their waistlines. Studies show that people with waistlines that measure more than thirty-six inches have a significantly greater risk of developing diabetes than people with smaller waistlines. These people appear to have round, apple-shaped bodies. Scientists believe that people with this body type are more insulin resistant than people with pear-shaped bodies. They do not know why this is so, but theorize that large quantities of centrally distributed fat cause more insulin resistance than fat in other areas.

Another group, people with family members who have diabetes, is also considered to be at risk. Because diabetes appears to run in families, many experts think that the susceptibility to developing the disorder is inherited. Studies have shown that the more relatives with diabetes a person has, the greater that person's chances of developing the disease. According to one study, children in families where one parent has diabetes have a 10 percent chance of developing the disease. Children's chances rise to 20 percent if both parents have diabetes, and to 40 percent if a brother or sister also has the disease. Similarly, a study of identical twins found that in more than 50 percent of the cases, when one twin was afflicted with diabetes the other twin had it too. A relative of a diabetic explains: "My mother-in-law has had diabetes for more than thirty years. She had a twin who died of diabetic complications. Everyone in her family has diabetes. Her sister is blind because of diabetes. Her cousin lost her leg to diabetes. She tries to take care of herself. She has to."[9]

Certain ethnic groups are also at high risk. Among these are African Americans, Hispanics, and Native Americans. Approximately 13 percent of all African Americans, about 2.8 million, have diabetes. These numbers climb as African Americans age. Twenty-five percent of African Americans over sixty-five years old have diabetes. African Americans are two times more likely than whites to have diabetes. The same is true for Hispanics. About 2 million Hispanics have diabetes. Although scientists do not know why diabetes is so prevalent in African Americans and Hispanics, they theorize that people in these groups inherit the tendency to develop diabetes.

Native Americans are at a higher risk of developing diabetes than any other ethnic group. Fifteen percent of all Native Americans over nineteen years old have diabetes. However, in some Native American tribes, diabetes has reached epidemic proportions. The Pima Indians of Arizona are the most common example. More than 50 percent of the adults over thirty years old in that tribe have diabetes. Some scientists believe that because many Native American tribes were confronted by food scarcities in the past, over time they developed genes to help their bodies to store and retain glucose for use during periods of famine. However, when food is plentiful this ability to store glucose causes blood sugar levels to soar. As a result, the pancreas cannot produce enough insulin, and diabetes develops.

Like this woman amputee, a quarter of all elderly African Americans have diabetes.

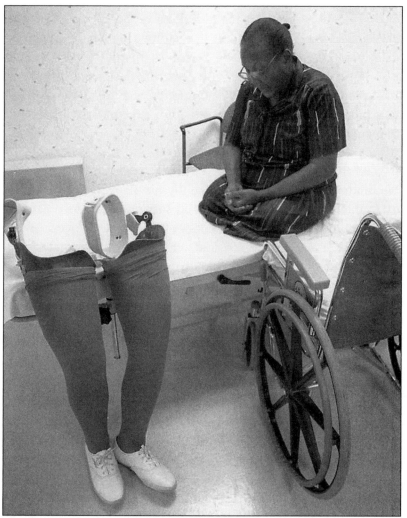

How Many People Are Affected?

Although people in higher risk groups may be more likely to develop diabetes, no one is immune to the disease. It affects people of all races and age groups. More than 17 million Americans, about 6.2 percent of the total population, have diabetes. Of these approximately 7.8 million are adult males, 9 million are adult females and 1 million are children. These numbers climb as people age. Of the 16 million adults who have diabetes, 7 million are over the age of 65. Scientists think that the reason the incidence of diabetes is so high in the elderly is that as people age their bodies become more resistant to insulin. This results in the development of type II diabetes. Scientists do not understand why insulin resistance increases with age. However, since people are living longer and the elderly population is expected to continue to grow, the incidence of diabetes among the elderly is expected to increase accordingly.

Physical Effects of Diabetes

No matter who gets diabetes, the disease has a powerful physical impact on the body. Excess blood sugar has a widespread and debilitating effect. Scientists believe that excess glucose in the bloodstream attaches to red and white blood cells, making the cells sticky. This causes the blood to thicken and clot and prevents the cells from performing their normal functions. For example, when glucose attaches to red blood cells, it uses up oxygen that red blood cells normally carry to the body. Over time, this lack of oxygen can cause blood vessels and nerves to narrow. This makes it difficult for the thickened blood to pass through them. Without an adequate blood supply, medical problems, or long-term complications of diabetes, can develop throughout the body. These complications include eye, kidney, heart, nerve, and foot problems.

Eye Problems

Problems in the eyes of people with diabetes are known as diabetic retinopathy. Diabetic retinopathy occurs when small blood

A doctor checks a diabetes patient's eyes for signs of damage to blood vessels, which can harm her eyesight.

vessels behind a part of the eye known as the retina narrow and close off. This stops the flow of blood to the eyes. In response, new blood vessels begin to grow. Frequently, the new blood vessels pull on the retina and cause it to detach. This often leads to blindness.

Diabetes is the leading cause of blindness in the United States. Each year about twenty-four thousand Americans become blind because of diabetes. A patient talks about his experience: "In 1989, I started having diabetic retinopathy, abnormal blood vessel growth in my right eye. That made me take my diabetes more seriously. . . . But the retinopathy, a common complication of diabetes, continued to progress. I had innumerable laser treatments and four surgeries to treat the condition, and hopefully save my sight. They were unsuccessful, and in late 1997 I became totally blind."[10]

Kidney Problems

Complications can also occur in the kidneys of people with diabetes when small blood vessels called capillaries, which filter waste from the blood into the urine, narrow. This causes waste to build up in the blood, which causes the kidneys to work harder. Over time, the stress of overwork causes the kidneys to fail. Diabetes is the leading cause of kidney disease in the United States. About 30 percent of people with type I diabetes and 10 percent of people with type II diabetes develop end-stage kidney disease, a condition where patients must undergo special treatment known as dialysis or receive a kidney transplant in order to live.

Kidney disease takes a number of years to develop in diabetics. As a result, many people with diabetes are surprised to find out they have contracted it. A patient with kidney disease caused by diabetes explains: "I was kind of shocked to find out I had kidney disease. I was just dealing with the diabetes. I never put the two together. If I had known that diabetes could damage my kidneys, I would have taken better care of myself."[11]

Problems in the Heart and Brain

Diabetes often affects the body's circulatory system. Because diabetes can cause arteries and veins throughout the body to narrow, blood flow to the heart and brain can be cut off. When this happens in arteries surrounding the heart, the result is a heart attack. When blood vessels around the brain are affected, a stroke occurs.

According to the National Institutes of Health, people with diabetes are four times more likely to have a heart attack or stroke than nondiabetics, and they are less likely to recover. For example, when nondiabetics have a heart attack, 15 percent die. But when diabetics have a heart attack 40 percent do not recover. The death rate is highest for diabetics with the highest blood glucose levels. Scientists believe this may be due to glucose attaching to white blood cells and weakening the body's ability to heal.

For those diabetics who do recover, the threat of a second heart attack is significantly higher than for nondiabetics. Diabetics suffer from a second heart attack more than 50 percent of the time; this occurs 25 percent of the time in nondiabetics. Making matters worse, when diabetics have a second heart attack 85 percent die within five years.

Damage to the Nervous System

Just as high blood sugar damages blood vessels, it has a similar effect on the nervous system. Lack of sufficient blood and oxygen caused by high blood glucose destroys nerve fiber and fat that insulates the nerves. As a result, the nerves that normally alert the body to pain, cold, and heat, do not receive proper signals. This causes some people with diabetes to either lose sensation or feel burning, tingling, and persistent pain wherever the nerves are affected. This condition is known as diabetic neuropathy.

About 65 percent of all people with diabetes develop diabetic neuropathy. In its most severe forms, when it is combined with narrowed blood vessels in the legs, it can lead to serious problems in diabetics' feet.

Because of nerve damage, many people with diabetes lose feeling in their feet. They may not feel a pebble in their shoe or a small sore or blister on their feet. As a result, they may walk on an injury. This can cause an infection to develop. Once an infection develops, it often becomes difficult to heal because narrowed blood vessels prohibit adequate blood from reaching

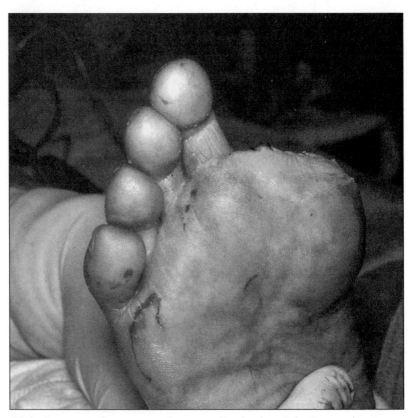

Diabetic neuropathy, or nerve damage, often leads to infections and eventually amputations of the lower extremities.

the wound. Consequently, infection-fighting white blood cells are unable to do their job. When this happens, the infection cannot be controlled and can spread throughout the foot, and even into the leg. The only way to stop the infection from spreading is by amputating, or removing, the affected limb.

About eighty-two thousand people with diabetes have feet or legs amputated each year. Most of these begin with minor foot wounds. Dr. Neil M. Scheffler talks about one of his patients:

> Mrs. Connell's little toe on her left foot had a large sore in it with something white in the center. The end of the toe was dark—black, really. The area around her toe was red. And the redness had spread to the middle of her foot. Mrs. Connell's

daughter had put a small dressing on the toe and this had drainage on it. When I touched the area, pus came out of the opening. Mrs. Connell was in trouble. She had a corn on that toe that had become infected. The white material that was exposed was the bone of the toe and the bone was infected. The end of the toe was gangrenous—the tissue was dead—and the infection had spread to her foot. . . . I knew that at least the toe would have to be removed.[12]

Short-Term Complications

Even when long-term complications are avoided, high blood glucose and lack of insulin can cause a dangerous, and sometimes deadly, short-term complication known as diabetes ketoacidosis or DKA. Diabetes ketoacidosis occurs when lack of insulin keeps glucose from entering and fueling the cells. As a result, the body breaks down fat for energy. When fat is burned in this way it produces a by-product known as ketones that build up in the blood and form a dangerous acid.

Diabetes ketoacidosis most often occurs in people with type I diabetes who neglect to take their daily insulin shots. However, stress can also lead to DKA. This is because the body normally releases sugar when it is under stress. Diabetes expert Dr. Abbas E. Kitabchi explains:

> When you're stressed, your body wants to make sugar available to your brain. It's a primitive response so that you can think and get away from whatever the danger is. Just to make sure the brain has enough fuel, your liver starts releasing glycogen. In someone who doesn't have diabetes, this isn't such a bad thing. The body just makes more insulin to handle the extra sugar. But if you have diabetes, that doesn't happen.[13]

Whether DKA is caused by stress or a forgotten insulin shot, it can make diabetics feel nauseated, confused, short of breath, and tired. If left untreated, it can result in a coma and death. Consequently, diabetes ketoacidosis is considered a diabetic emergency. Patients with DKA are hospitalized and treated with insulin. Fortunately, most patients recuperate within twenty-four hours.

It is clear that diabetes has a powerful impact on the body. High blood glucose and lack of insulin can cause troubling short- and long-term complications in the millions of people who suffer from this widespread disease.

Chapter 2

Diagnosis and Treatment

D IABETES IS NOT difficult to diagnose. However, the two types of diabetes sometimes show different symptoms. The symptoms of type II diabetes, for instance, often take a long time to develop and can be so mild that patients mistake them for other problems such as fatigue or a mild infection. Consequently, many people with type II diabetes do not undergo testing. This is usually not the case in type I diabetes, however. Type I diabetes symptoms usually begin suddenly and can be quite severe. A patient explains: "One Sunday morning I was so weak I couldn't deliver my newspapers. I was taken to the family doctor and then rushed right into the hospital. I was very ill. So ill, I couldn't hold my head up. My doctor came into the room and talked to me. He said I had a disease called diabetes."[14]

Symptoms

Whether symptoms begin gradually or suddenly, once they appear, doctors often suspect the cause is diabetes. Symptoms of diabetes include frequent urination, unusual thirst and hunger, weight loss, and fatigue. Frequent urination occurs when diabetics' kidneys try to flush excess glucose out of their bloodstreams. As a result, their bladders become fuller than normal causing them to have to urinate frequently. Frequent urination eliminates large quantities of water. Because the body needs to replace water lost in urinating, diabetics feel thirsty most of the time and drink frequently. A patient talks about his experience:

Diabetes Symptoms

- Frequent urination (even at night)
- Excessive thirst
- Dry skin
- Slow healing of cuts
- Blurry eyesight
- Always being very hungry
- Feeling tired and weak
- Weight loss
- Skin infections
- Numbness or tingling in feet

"My family decided to move to Denver. We traveled to Denver a couple of times in search of a house. Because of my rapidly escalating symptoms each trip was a nightmare. On the way to Colorado, we stopped every half-hour so I could use the rest room. I waited until I was about to burst and then we would stop; a half-hour later we would repeat the process."[15]

Unusual hunger and fatigue are also symptoms of diabetes. Lack of insulin keeps glucose from entering the cells and providing diabetics with energy. Consequently, people with diabetes feel tired and become increasingly hungry as their bodies become deprived of fuel. This causes people with diabetes to eat more than usual.

However, even though they are eating more, many diabetics lose weight. This is because without sufficient insulin, diabetics cannot use the glucose in the food they eat for fuel. Instead, their bodies break down muscle and fat tissue to provide their cells with energy. A patient talks about her experience: "I had a tremendous appetite. My son said he'd never seen anyone eat the way I was eating. I ate three meals a day, and snacked continuously. But my clothes just kept getting bigger and bigger on me. It was like I was shrinking. I went to the doctor. He said it was all because of my blood sugar."[16]

Testing

Although symptoms like frequent urination, excess hunger and thirst, weight loss, and fatigue point to diabetes, the only way to diagnose diabetes accurately is through blood tests that measure blood glucose levels. Doctors use two blood tests to do this. In the first, called a random plasma glucose test, the

A nurse takes a blood sample to test for diabetes, which is diagnosed by analyzing blood glucose levels.

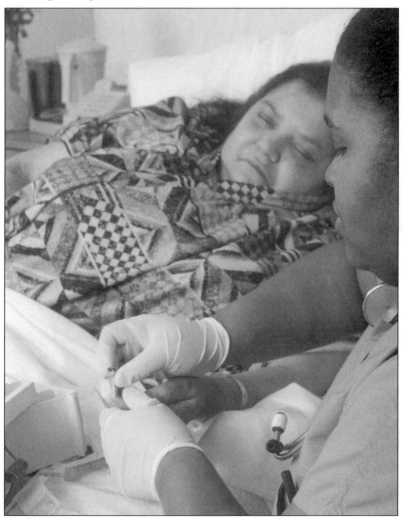

doctor withdraws a small sample of the patient's blood from a vein in his or her arm. The withdrawn blood is usually sent to a laboratory where it is analyzed and the level of blood glucose is measured. Normal blood glucose levels on the random plasma glucose test range from 60 to 140 milligrams. When blood glucose levels are 200 milligrams or more, diabetes is indicated.

However, since a random blood glucose test can be taken at any time, if patients have recently eaten a sugary meal that could cause their blood glucose levels to rise, the test results may be abnormally high. Consequently, when the result of a patient's random plasma glucose test is high, doctors usually administer a second test to verify the diagnosis. This test is known as a fasting plasma glucose test. It is administered in the same way as the random plasma glucose test, but it is given to patients after they have fasted for eight to twelve hours. Since everyone's blood glucose normally falls after fasting, experts consider a fasting plasma glucose test to be the most accurate test for diagnosing diabetes. Normally, blood glucose levels are no higher than 115 milligrams after fasting. However, because insufficient insulin or insulin resistance keeps blood glucose from entering diabetics' cells, even after fasting, diabetics' blood glucose levels usually are well above 115 milligrams.

Type I or Type II

Once a diagnosis indicates that the patient has diabetes, to treat the disease effectively, the doctor must determine whether the patient has type I or type II diabetes. To do this, the doctor looks at a number of factors including the patient's age, since most cases of type I diabetes begin before age forty. Conversely, when patients are over forty, type II diabetes is indicated.

Another important factor is the patient's weight. People with type I diabetes are usually thin or average weight. On the other hand, obesity is a common characteristic of people with type II diabetes. Even though diabetes can cause people to lose weight, if a patient is currently overweight, or has been overweight in the past, the patient is probably suffering from type II diabetes.

Doctors also look at blood glucose levels to determine which type of diabetes patients have. Because people with type I diabetes do not produce any insulin, their blood glucose levels are usually higher than that of people with type II diabetes. The average blood glucose levels of type I diabetics are more than 300 milligrams; they usually range from 200 to 250 milligrams in people with type II diabetes. A mother of a son with type I diabetes recalls the results of her son Lyle's first blood glucose test: "The doctor did a random blood glucose [test] which was 468 milligrams. A repeat random blood glucose test was 392 milligrams. Lyle has type 1 diabetes."[17]

Once the doctor determines which type of diabetes the patient has, a treatment plan that includes medication, diet, and exercise is prescribed. Although different medications are used to treat type I and type II diabetes, all treatment focuses on normalizing the patients' blood glucose levels. This is achieved by balancing insulin and blood glucose levels.

Treatment with Insulin

Medication is the primary form of treatment for diabetes, but the type and strength of medication depends on the type of diabetes patients have. Type I diabetics usually are treated with insulin to substitute for the insulin their bodies cannot manufacture. Without insulin diabetics cannot survive.

In the past, insulin used to treat diabetics was extracted from cows and pigs. However, scientists have learned to synthetically produce human insulin. Combining the human insulin gene with harmless bacteria does this. The result is a man-made form of insulin that is almost the same as the insulin produced by the pancreas. Because insulin is a protein, if it is taken orally the body breaks it down like protein in food rather than sending it to the cells where it is needed. For this reason, insulin must be injected to be effective.

There are four types of insulin: rapid-acting insulin, short-acting insulin, intermediate-acting insulin, and long-acting insulin. They are all designed to maintain a balance between blood glucose levels and insulin levels. But they differ in their

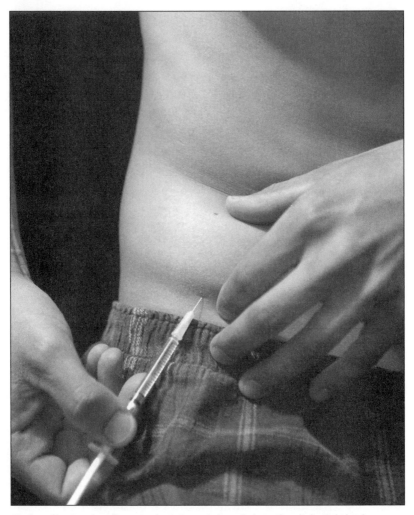

To be effective, insulin must be injected directly into the diabetic's body.

onset (how quickly they start working), their peak time (when they work the hardest), and their duration (how long they last in the body). Since every person is different and insulin levels normally rise and fall depending on when and what people eat, their physical activity, and their stress level, each person's response to insulin is different.

In order to match their insulin levels to their blood glucose levels, most diabetics take a combination of at least two types of insulin each day. The number of injections and the type of insulin diabetics use depend on their blood sugar levels. However, since blood sugar generally rises after eating, most people with diabetes inject themselves before every meal. A patient explains: "I inject myself six or seven times daily using two types of insulin. One is called Humulin and it is long-acting insulin that takes effect in about four hours and lasts twelve hours. The other is called Humulog and it is fast acting. It takes effect in about fifteen minutes and lasts two hours, almost like a real pancreas."[18]

Insulin Shots

There are a number of different tools that people can use to get insulin into their bodies. A syringe and needle are the most common. When patients are diagnosed with diabetes, their doctor usually teaches them how to cleanse the injection sight, fill the syringe with the proper dose of insulin, and inject themselves. Although taking shots can be unpleasant, most patients find that specially designed microfine needles help make the process less painful, as does injecting the insulin into a fatty part of the body such as the abdomen, thighs, buttocks, or upper arms. This also prevents problems that can occur when insulin is injected into a muscle, which is painful and causes the insulin to start working too quickly.

Although many patients find injecting themselves with a needle frightening at first, most diabetics realize that these injections are lifesavers, and adjust to the process. A patient talks about his experience: "[At first] I hated the needles, but . . . I came to realize the needle I hated would give me life. I'm actually grateful for the injections I have to take twice everyday. If someone had not had the ingenuity to come up with a method for the transfer of insulin from one body to the next, I would not be here."[19]

Insulin Pens

Insulin pens are another tool patients use to inject themselves with insulin. Insulin pens are small and portable. They look like a ballpoint pen with a thin disposable needle on the tip. Rather than being filled with an ink cartridge, insulin pens are filled with a cartridge of insulin. To use an insulin pen, patients insert the cartridge into the pen, stick the needle into their skin, and press a button on the side of the pen to inject the insulin. Because insulin pens are so small and resemble real pens, many patients feel comfortable using them in public. A patient explains: "I need to inject away from home a lot. The convenience is marvelous."[20]

This young diabetic injects herself with insulin using a convenient "pen."

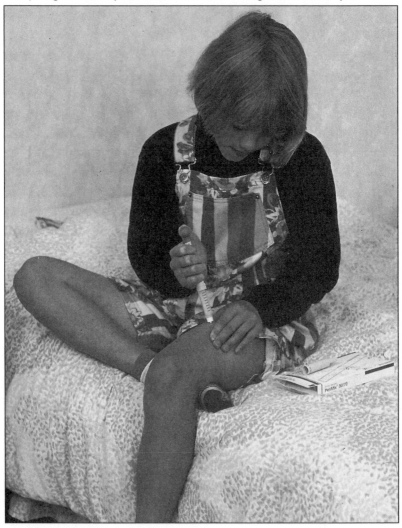

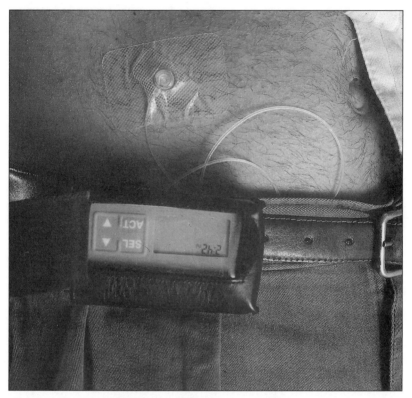

Resembling an ordinary beeper, this pump delivers a regular dose of insulin to this diabetic through the attached tube and needle.

Jet Injectors and Insulin Pumps

Jet injectors are another insulin delivery tool. They do not contain a needle. This makes them popular with people who have problems with needles. Somewhat larger than a syringe, a jet injector works by sending a premeasured dose of insulin directly into the patient through the use of a high pressure air mechanism that acts like a liquid needle.

Like jet injectors, insulin pumps are popular with people who prefer not to use a syringe. Insulin pumps are the newest type of insulin delivery tool. Insulin pumps look like pagers. They are small, lightweight, computerized machines that are filled with insulin and connected to a narrow tube that ends with a needle. Patients wear the pump around their waist or in their pocket with the needle inserted in their skin. The pump releases a slow steady dose of insulin through the tube into the patient's body. An alarm in the pump alerts the user when the pump needs to be refilled. Patients can push a button on the pump when they need more insulin, such as before meals. A mother of a diabetic who uses the pump talks about her son's experience: "Management of his illness is a little easier now that he uses the pump instead of syringes. The pump simulates the workings of a real pancreas, delivering insulin through a catheter [tube] in his side. It's a steadier more reliable delivery system than a syringe and it's easier for him to use."[21]

Oral Medication

Since people with type II diabetes produce some insulin, they usually do not need to take additional insulin. Instead, they are treated with medication that helps their bodies produce more insulin, or better utilize the insulin they do produce. Usually taken in pill form once or twice a day, this medication includes three families of drugs: sulfonylurea, glitazone, and metaformin.

Although all three medications lower blood glucose levels, they each work in a different way. Sulfonylurea, the oldest type of medication for type II diabetes, lowers blood glucose levels by encouraging the pancreas to produce and release more insulin. It does this because it contains sulphur, a chemical that stimulates beta cells to manufacture insulin. Glitazone works by reversing insulin resistance. The chemicals that make up glitazone cause changes in fat and muscle cells throughout the body. These changes allow insulin to enter the cells, reducing blood glucose levels. And metaformin, the newest type of diabetes medication, blocks cells in the liver from releasing glycogen, a form of glucose. By blocking glycogen from being released into the bloodstream, metaformin lowers blood glucose levels. A patient talks about his experience with metaformin: "I take [metaformin] twice a day. It has really helped me. Without it, my sugar level would be in the 400 plus range; with it my sugar level stays between 120 and 150 and I feel so much better."[22]

Risks and Side Effects of Medication

Despite the benefits of diabetes medications, there are health risks and side effects as with any drugs. Among the most troubling is the problem caused when diabetes medication causes blood sugar levels to fall below 70 milligrams, leading to a dangerous condition known as hypoglycemia, or insulin reaction. Hypoglycemia usually occurs when patients take too much insulin or oral medication. It also can arise when patients eat too little or exercise aggressively, which causes their normal dose of insulin to be absorbed more quickly, allowing glucose to enter the cells faster the usual. Unless patients adjust their medication accordingly, this lowers the balance between glucose and insulin and causes blood sugar levels to drop.

People with type II diabetes produce some insulin and take oral medication like these tablets to maximize their bodies' function.

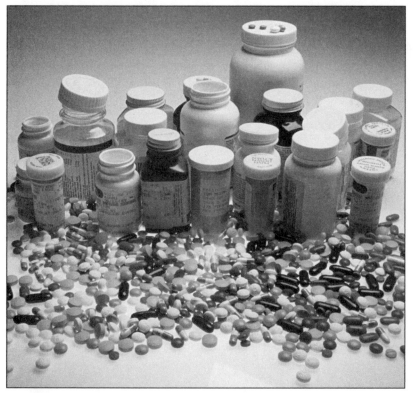

The symptoms of hypoglycemia come on suddenly and include cold sweats, weakness, rapid heartbeat, irritability, and hunger. Lack of glucose reaching the brain causes confusion, personality changes, blurred vision, seizures, and unconsciousness. If left untreated, hypoglycemia can result in the patient going into a coma, and can cause death. Diabetes expert Sue K. Milchovich recalls one of her patients' experiences: "Jake felt himself becoming very irritated. A few minutes later he became shaky and nervous and broke out in a cold sweat. Immediately his thoughts flashed back to his half eaten lunch, his usual dose of insulin, and the extra exercise he was getting. Insulin reaction, he thought."[23]

Diet

Diet is another important part of diabetes treatment. Because food produces glucose, when and what a person eats has a direct impact on the balance between blood glucose and insulin. Consequently, people with diabetes must pay attention to the type of food they eat and when they eat it. In order to balance blood glucose levels with medication and avoid hypoglycemia, people with diabetes should not skip meals. They need to eat on a regular schedule that corresponds with when they take their medication. This usually involves eating three meals and several snacks a day.

What diabetics eat is just as important as when they eat. People with diabetes have the same nutritional needs as nondiabetics. That is why the American Diabetes Association advises people with diabetes to eat a wide variety of foods based on the food pyramid, the same diet system that is suggested for all Americans. According to diabetes expert Diane Guagliani, "There is no difference between the way someone with diabetes should eat and the way the rest of us should. People with diabetes should eat a well-balanced diet from a wide variety of foods that's low in fat and supplies adequate nutrients."[24]

Foods in the food pyramid are divided into seven sections with recommended daily serving amounts. Foods such as bread, cereal, and pasta that are found at the widest part of the pyramid

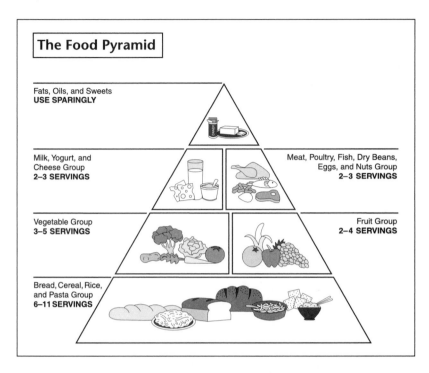

The Food Pyramid

Fats, Oils, and Sweets
USE SPARINGLY

Milk, Yogurt, and
Cheese Group
2–3 SERVINGS

Meat, Poultry, Fish, Dry Beans,
Eggs, and Nuts Group
2–3 SERVINGS

Vegetable Group
3–5 SERVINGS

Fruit Group
2–4 SERVINGS

Bread, Cereal, Rice,
and Pasta Group
6–11 SERVINGS

have the most nutritional value and correspondingly, the highest amount of daily recommended servings. Conversely, foods such as sweets and fats that are found at the tip of the pyramid have the lowest nutritional value and the lowest amount of recommended daily servings. Following the food pyramid upward from the widest level, the American Diabetes Association recommends that diabetics eat six to eleven servings of whole grains such as bread, cereal, and pasta each day; three to five servings of vegetables; two to four servings of fruit; two to three servings of meat, fish, eggs, and beans; two to three servings of milk products; and infrequent servings of sweets and fats. A patient talks about his diet: "I eat a balanced diet every day. That's a burger with a green vegetable instead of fries at lunch, a small breakfast, and a big salad and meat or chicken at dinner. I know if I eat this way, I'm actually eating the way everyone should."[25]

It is also important that diabetics eat some food from each group at each meal. This is because the body changes carbohydrates, found in foods such as whole grains and fruits, into glucose within one hour of their being eaten. Protein found in milk products, meat, beans, and fish is changed into glucose more slowly. As a result, when protein and carbohydrates are combined, the protein keeps blood sugar from rising too quickly. This helps to maintain a balance between blood glucose and insulin levels. A patient talks about how this affects him: "My glucose goes up when I eat a simple meal like a bowl of cornflakes. It stays lower even if I eat a pepperoni pizza, because the pizza has protein in the cheese and meat that balances the carbohydrates in the crust and sauce. That keeps my glucose levels down."[26]

Exercise

The third component of diabetes treatment is exercise. Exercise is very important in normalizing blood glucose levels. When people exercise, their muscle cells need more glucose for energy. As a result, the exerciser's heart beats rapidly causing more blood to circulate through the body. This causes more insulin and more glucose to reach the cells. In addition, during exercise muscle cells become more sensitive to insulin, which makes them need less insulin in order to open their walls to let glucose in. This helps diabetics to better balance insulin and glucose and to lower glucose levels in the bloodstream. According to sports medicine expert Dr. Warren A. Scott, "Think of an exercising muscle as being a glucose sponge. Vigorous exercise can cause muscles to increase glucose uptake as much as twentyfold, acting much like insulin in getting muscle cells to open up their glucose doors."[27]

What is more, muscle cells retain their sensitivity to insulin for about two days after people exercise. So when people with diabetes exercise regularly, their cells need less insulin to utilize glucose, resulting in less glucose in their blood. The effect of exercise, then, allows many diabetics to decrease their dosage of insulin or oral medication. Diabetes expert Porter Shimer explains: "Exercise can be so effective in its insulin-like action, in fact, that it can help many people with type 2 diabetes eliminate their needs for medication entirely, while for those with type 1 diabetes it can reduce their insulin needs by as much as 50 percent."[28]

In addition to lowering blood glucose levels, exercise also has other health benefits. Exercise strengthens the heart and circulatory system. This lessens diabetics' risk of heart attacks and strokes. Exercise increases the circulation of blood and oxygen throughout the body. This helps get more blood to diabetics' feet where complications often arise. Moreover, because exercise causes the body to release endorphins, natural chemicals that give the exerciser a feeling of well-being, it helps lessen the

Exercise such as running is an effective way to normalize blood glucose levels.

tingling, pain, and burning caused by diabetic neuropathy. Dr. Scott explains: "Exercise gives people a sense of empowerment over their disease. It makes them look better and feel better too. In all the years I've worked with this disease, I'm still amazed at how much better patients do when they make regular exercise an important part of their lives."[29]

Consequently, many diabetics find that following a treatment plan that combines exercise, a healthy diet, and medication helps them control the symptoms of diabetes and lessens their risk of developing complications. This greatly improves their lives.

Chapter 3

Alternative and Complementary Treatment

CONVENTIONAL TREATMENT FOR diabetes focuses solely on balancing insulin and glucose levels. However, diabetes causes problems throughout the body and managing the disease can be difficult. The result is often mental and physical stress. In order to relieve stress, avoid physical complications, and better control diabetes, many diabetics combine conventional treatments with alternative treatments.

What Are Alternative and Complementary Treatments?

An alternative treatment is a treatment or therapy that is not widely accepted by the traditional medical community in the United States. Some forms of alternative treatments such as acupuncture, meditation, and yoga have been widely studied; others have not. Unlike conventional treatments, which are subjected to rigorous testing before being approved by the Food and Drug Administration, a U.S. government agency that sets standards and regulates medication, many alternative treatments undergo only limited testing. In fact, the U.S. government does not regulate alternative treatments at all. This can be harmful since the government establishes that the benefits of conventional treatments exceed any potential risks before they can be prescribed. This is not the case with alternative treatments. In addition, some alternative treatments employ anecdotal evidence, using patients' testimony as proof of the treatment's effectiveness. However, anecdotal evidence does not include a control group, rarely reports any negative results, and does not survey enough subjects to be scientifically sound.

Despite those concerns, many health care professionals believe that when alternative treatments are combined with conventional drug treatments, in a method known as complementary treatment, they can be effective in treating diabetes. A survey conducted by the *Diabetes Educator*, a journal for health care professionals, reported that 63 percent of diabetes health care professionals recommend complementary treatment to their patients. Doctors suggest complementary treatment because it can increase relaxation and lower stress levels, reduce pain from diabetic neuropathy, and help patients better manage diabetes symptoms, making them feel more in control of their lives. A doctor explains why she refers diabetes patients to alternative therapists: "Traditional medicine doesn't have all the answers. Alternative therapies offer hope for a lot of people."[30]

Dietary Treatments

The most widely used and accepted alternative treatments for diabetes fall into three categories: dietary treatments that focus on lowering blood glucose, mind-body treatments that promote relaxation and lower stress, and physical treatments that seek to prevent diabetic complications. Of these, dietary treatments are the most popular.

Alternative diets for diabetes are more restrictive than those that follow the food pyramid. Alternative diets focus on the quality of food eaten and prohibit the consumption of certain foods, which experts believe are unhealthy. A vegetarian diet, for example, is a popular alternative diet for diabetes.

People who follow a vegetarian diet do not eat meat, and some do not eat any food that comes from animals. This includes fish, chicken, eggs, and often milk products. Instead, vegetarians eat a diet rich in vegetables, fruit, whole grains, nuts, and beans. Vegetarian diets are high in natural fiber,

Many diabetics find that vegetarian diets improve their health and sense of well-being.

which because of its bulk, is believed to slow down food digestion and the resulting release of glucose into the bloodstream. This helps lower blood glucose levels. Vegetarian diets are also low in fat, which helps overweight people with diabetes lose weight. A study conducted in 1999 at Georgetown University in

Washington, D.C. compared fasting blood glucose levels of diabetics who ate a strict vegetarian diet for three months to those who ate a balanced diet that followed the food pyramid. The study found that after three months the vegetarians' fasting blood glucose levels had fallen by 28 percent, versus a 12 percent decrease for the nonvegetarians. In addition, the vegetarians lost an average of sixteen pounds, double the loss of the other subjects. The subjects on a vegetarian diet also lowered their blood cholesterol levels, helping to lower their risk of heart and circulatory problems, and lowered the amount of protein in their urine, which when high, contributes to kidney problems. As a result, several of the vegetarian subjects were able to reduce their daily medication. According to the American Dietetic Association, "Scientific data suggests a positive relationship between a vegetarian diet and reduced risk for several chronic diseases including diabetes. It is the position of the American Dietetic Association that appropriately planned vegetarian diets are healthful, are nutritionally adequate, and provide health benefits in the prevention and treatment of certain diseases." [31]

The Atkins Diet

Another popular alternative diet for diabetes is a high fat, low carbohydrate diet known as the Atkins diet. Developed by Dr. Robert Atkins, the Atkins diet prohibits the consumption of all carbohydrates including bread, cereal, rice, potatoes, pasta, and fruits, and prohibits dieters from eating anything containing sugar or white flour. Instead dieters eat foods high in fat and protein such as meats, butter, eggs, and cheese.

Because carbohydrates are turned into glucose rapidly, and fats and proteins are turned into glucose slowly, Dr. Atkins believes that replacing carbohydrates with fats and proteins lowers blood glucose and keeps it from fluctuating. According to Dr. Atkins, "We've got real human beings who have been on this diet, and they'll tell you exactly what happens. They've never felt better in their life. If they have medical problems such as diabetes, their need for medication goes away." [32]

Nutritional Supplements

Other alternative dietary treatments for diabetes combine the food pyramid diet with nutritional supplements. Among the most popular are antioxidants. Antioxidants are substances that strengthen the body by fighting against free radicals, chemicals that weaken the body and cause disease. Many experts believe that free radicals help glucose to stick to red blood cells and damage insulin-producing beta cells in the pancreas. Antioxidants

Dr. Robert Atkins is known for developing the no carbohydrate Atkins diet that many diabetics follow.

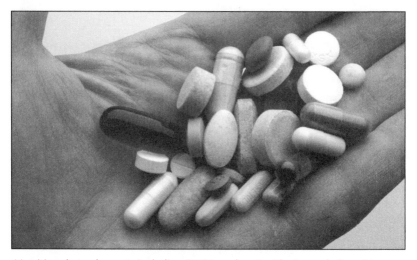

Nutritional supplements including DHEA and antioxidants are believed to improve the body's utilization of glucose.

such as alpha-lipoic acid and vitamins A, B, C, and E counter the effect of free radicals. Consequently, many people with diabetes take a variety of different antioxidants in an effort to prevent damage from free radicals and to decrease the risk of diabetic complications such as kidney disease and diabetic neuropathy.

By preventing glucose from sticking to red blood cells, alpha-lipoic acid, in particular, is believed to increase blood flow to the legs and feet of diabetics. A study in Germany measured the results of treatment with alpha-lipoic acid on diabetics who suffered from diabetic neuropathy. After three weeks, the patients had better blood flow and increased feeling in their feet. Another study conducted in 1997 in the Mayo Clinic in the United States had similar results. As a result of these and other studies, alpha-lipoic acid is commonly used as a treatment for diabetic neuropathy in Europe. A patient who takes alpha-lipoic acid explains: "I've done really great on this. . . . I've had diabetes for two years now. I feel very good. I have not had any complications from my diabetes."[33]

Another popular nutritional supplement for diabetes is dehydroepiandrosterone, or DHEA. DHEA is a hormone that is naturally produced in the human body. Its production peaks when people are around thirty years old and decreases as people age. Levels of DHEA also decrease when people are sick. Although scientists are unsure what DHEA's job is in the body, people who take DHEA to treat diabetes believe that it improves the body's ability to use glucose and is important in insulin production. A study in 1994 examined DHEA levels in diabetics and nondiabetics. The study found lower than normal DHEA levels in the diabetics. An earlier study, in 1991, found that subjects with low levels of DHEA tend to be overweight and do not use glucose effectively. Other research using animals found that treating overweight animals with DHEA caused them to lose weight. Consequently, many diabetics use DHEA to help them lose weight and better utilize their blood glucose.

Herbs

Herbs are a common and ancient alternative treatment for diabetes. Herbal remedies use the leaves, stems, and roots of certain plants that are known to have healing properties. From medieval times until the twentieth century, when other medicines were developed, doctors prescribed more than four hundred different herbal remedies in tea or pill form as a primary treatment for diabetes. In fact, a mixture of herbal extracts with chemicals makes up one-fourth of all conventional medicines prescribed today. Metaformin, for example, uses ingredients from rue and French lilac, two herbs, in combination with chemicals.

Since herbal remedies use only natural plant parts, users feel that they are gentler than traditional medicine. About one-third of all adults in the United States have used herbal remedies. Although no herb can substitute for insulin, studies have shown that a number of herbs have a positive effect on blood glucose and other symptoms of diabetes. Among these are gymnema and ginseng.

Gymnema comes from India, and its name in Hindi, an Indian language, means "sugar destroyer." It has been used in Asia for centuries to treat diabetes. In a number of tests gymnema has been shown to lower blood glucose levels of people with diabetes. It does this by increasing insulin production. One study in

India compared the blood glucose levels of subjects who were treated with gymnema and insulin for thirty months with that of subjects who were treated with insulin alone. The study found that the blood glucose levels of the group who received the combined treatment dropped from an average of 232 milligrams to 152 milligrams. As a result, these patients were able to drop their daily insulin dose by 50 percent. The group treated with insulin alone had no change in their blood glucose levels. Scientists are not sure how gymnema works. However, they hypothesize that acid found in gymnema's leaves and roots stimulates beta cells to produce more insulin.

Ginseng is another popular herb for treating diabetes. Commonly used in Chinese medicine as a tonic to strengthen the body and relieve stress, ginseng is also believed to lower blood glucose levels. A Canadian study in 2000 found that ginseng supplements lowered blood glucose levels by 20 percent in subjects with diabetes. Ginseng also has a stimulating effect on the body. It causes the heart to increase blood circulation and muscle cells to react in the same manner as to physical activity.

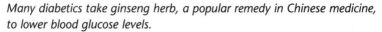

Many diabetics take ginseng herb, a popular remedy in Chinese medicine, to lower blood glucose levels.

Scientists speculate that this causes ginseng to lower insulin resistance in a manner similar to exercise. A patient who takes ginseng talks about its benefits:

> My doctor wanted me to take glucophage twice a day. But I'm a small person and I felt that two pills a day was too much. With just the one glucophage, I had trouble keeping my blood sugar down. I started taking a ginseng tablet too. Since I started, my sugar has dropped over fifty points and I feel stronger and have more energy. My doctor says that I've never been healthier.[34]

Mind-Body Treatments

Mind-body treatments are another popular alternative treatment. Popular mind-body treatments include meditation, yoga, and aromatherapy. These treatments focus on the connection between the mind and the body. By promoting a feeling of well-being they lower stress. This is important since stress causes blood glucose levels to rise. According to diabetes expert David Drum, "If you have diabetes, the regular practice of mind/body techniques may help lower blood sugar and pressure, increase blood circulation to extremities, combat depression and even assist in efforts to lose or maintain weight."[35]

Meditation

Meditation is one of the most widely researched alternative treatments for diabetes. In meditation, patients use concentration techniques such as silently repeating a word or a chant to clear the mind in order to relax the body and relieve stress. Research shows that levels of chemicals, such as adrenaline, which the body produces as a response to stress, decrease during meditation sessions. And these levels remain lowered when patients practice meditation often. This reduces levels of stress and anxiety that cause the body to release extra glucose into the bloodstream.

Although experts are unsure why meditation changes chemical levels in the body, the results are so impressive that many doctors and diabetics endorse using meditation as a treatment

Meditation is an alternative therapy that helps many diabetics cope with their illness.

for diabetes. A patient explains: "My job is stressful, and I've got a home and family. Add to the mix having diabetes, watching what I eat, taking medicine, and worrying about my blood sugar. If it weren't for the time I meditate every morning, I'd be a total mess. Meditation helps me to find some balance. It keeps me from stressing out and keeps my blood sugar down."[36]

Yoga

Yoga is also a widely used alternative treatment that relieves stress. Yoga is a form of exercise that originated in ancient India. It involves slow controlled stretching and breathing. This relaxes and strengthens the body while helping to reduce blood glucose levels by lowering stress. Because it is a form of exercise, yoga also improves blood circulation, allowing more insulin and glucose to reach the cells.

Thousands of research studies into the effectiveness of yoga have been done in India. One study conducted in 1993 compared the blood glucose levels of diabetics who practiced yoga to those who did not. The researchers found a significant reduction in the blood glucose levels of those who practiced yoga.

Yoga is a form of meditative exercise that relieves stress, in turn lowering blood glucose levels.

Aromatherapy

Aromatherapy is another treatment that people with diabetes find is effective in helping control their blood glucose levels by relieving stress. Aromatherapy is based on the theory that the sense of smell influences physical and psychological reactions. Consequently, it uses scent to improve mental and physical health and well-being.

In aromatherapy, diabetes patients inhale warmed oils derived from plants believed to have tranquilizing properties. These include lavender, chamomile, rose, and basil oil. Patients report that using these oils results in their feeling more relaxed. The oil is usually placed in a special electric diffuser or an aroma lamp. There it heats up and disperses into the air as a mist. Patients breathe in this mist, and the oil is absorbed into the bloodstream through the lungs. There, the mist acts as a relaxant. Research has shown that brain wave patterns are affected by scent, and that scent produces an emotional effect on patients. Consequently, when oils that have tranquilizing properties are used, they produce a calming effect on the patient. "I mix lavender and rose oils in my diffuser and let it run while I meditate," a patient who uses aromatherapy for diabetes explains. "The scent is wonderful, like a stroll through my grandma's garden. It relaxes and refreshes me. That has to help my diabetes."[37]

Acupuncture

Physical treatments also attempt to prevent or relieve the symptoms of complications from diabetes. Acupuncture, in particular, has been studied extensively by the National Institutes of Health, and has been found to relieve chronic pain. It is a popular treatment for pain, a common symptom of diabetic neuropathy. A complete understanding of why acupuncture relieves pain eludes experts. However, the most commonly accepted theory is that acupuncture causes a biological response that stimulates the body to produce endorphins, the body's natural painkiller. Recommended by the World Health Organization and the National Institutes of Health as a treatment for pain, acupuncture is offered in many pain clinics throughout the United States.

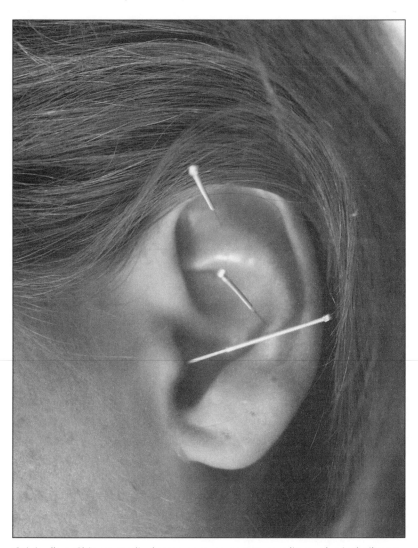

Originally a Chinese medical treatment, acupuncture relieves physical ailments such as complications of diabetes.

Acupuncture is an ancient form of Chinese medicine based on the theory that healthy people have a life-energy called chi flowing through their bodies; if this energy becomes blocked, illness and pain occur. Acupuncture involves inserting hair-thin needles into specific points in the body where acupuncturists believe energy channels are blocked. The needles are believed to stimulate the flow of energy through these points, thus relieving pain.

Despite the lack of evidence proving that these energy channels do exist, evidence has shown that acupuncture significantly reduces the pain of diabetic neuropathy. In fact, it has been shown to be so effective that, in an English study, 67 percent of diabetes patients taking pain medication for diabetic neuropathy were able to stop or reduce their medication after being treated with acupuncture for ten weeks. The scientists who conducted the study determined that acupuncture "is a safe and effective therapy for long-term management of painful diabetic neuropathy."[38]

Chelation Therapy

Chelation therapy is another physical treatment aimed at relieving complications caused by diabetes. Chelation therapy involves patients being given a man-made amino acid called EDTA or ethylene diamine tetra-acedic acid, intravenously. Also used to treat lead poisoning, EDTA is believed to attach to and remove minerals such as calcium and iron, which build up on the walls of narrowed arteries and veins. The body then excretes these minerals as waste. This permits blood to reach the feet and legs of diabetics.

There have not been many studies into the effectiveness of chelation therapy. However, in one study conducted by the American College of Advancement of Medicine, 197 of 200 diabetes patients who were facing limb amputation, due to blocked circulation, were able to save their legs after treatment with chelation therapy. Thus, many doctors endorse its use.

Controversial Treatments

As a result of the large number of people who seek help managing diabetes, a thriving industry offering alternative treatments for the disease has developed. Many of these treatments such as acupuncture and meditation have a long history of use and effectiveness and appear to offer patients relief. But the effectiveness and safety of other treatments, which have not been tested or used widely, are more controversial. Among the most controversial treatment methods are those that use questionable ingredients.

Treatment with dimethyl sulfoxide or DMSO, a powerful chemical used in paint thinner, falls into this category. When it is rubbed on wounds that will not heal due to diabetic neuropathy and circulatory problems, DMSO is believed to increase healing. There is little evidence that DMSO is effective, but in some cases treatment with it has been successful. Many experts believe that the relief DMSO gives patients is due to the placebo effect. This means the patients' strong belief that a treatment will work rather than the efficacy of the treatment results in success.

Risks and Side Effects of Alternative Treatment

Although many patients are turning to alternative treatments hoping to find a gentler and more effective way to manage diabetes, alternative treatments, like conventional treatments, can pose serious health risks. One of the greatest risks occurs when people replace conventional treatment with alternative treatment. Although alternative treatments may improve diabetes symptoms temporarily, they cannot replace treatment with insulin. Thus, relinquishing conventional treatment completely can be extremely dangerous. Without sufficient insulin, diabetics cannot survive.

Lack of regulations of many alternative products and lack of mandatory licensing of many alternative practitioners can also present health risks. Even seemingly harmless alternative treatments such as yoga can be hazardous if the instructor is not experienced in working with diabetics. Certain yoga exercises may be harmful to people with diabetes. For example, exercises that elevate the feet above the head increase blood pressure on blood vessels of the eye. This can worsen diabetic retinopathy, and even cause the retina to detach.

Other complications arise due to the lack of regulations of herbal products. Unlike the monitoring of conventional medicine in which government agencies supervise the level of active

ingredients, levels of active ingredients in herbs are not monitored, and there are no set dosage levels. Herbs may be too
strong, causing a bad reaction. There have been cases in which
the strength of herbal products has been found to be three times
the amount stated on the label. And high doses of popular herbs
used to treat diabetes such as ginseng and fenugreek can cause
hypoglycemia. Even worse, high doses of ackee fruit, a Jamaican

*The toxic Jamaican ackee fruit, believed to lower blood glucose levels,
has been liked to thousands of deaths.*

herb believed to lower blood glucose, is so toxic that more than five thousand deaths have been linked to its use. Accordingly, expert Bernadette Mariott warns: "There are a number of botanical supplements [herbs] that are marketed as helpful for diabetes, but we have very little data on these in terms of scientific clinical trials. In many cases the active ingredient of a particular herb is unknown—as are its potentially harmful side effects."[39]

Despite the dangers that alternative treatments can pose, many people with diabetes successfully combine alternative and conventional treatments. When used properly, such a combination can relieve stress, lessen long-term health risks, and make diabetics feel more in control of their lives. As one diabetes patient who successfully combines alternative and conventional treatment explains: "I take oral medication, carefully watch my diet, exercise, and I meditate and use aromatherapy. I feel like it's a good combination. I feel strong, healthy, and calm. Like I'm in charge, not my diabetes."[40]

Chapter 4

Living with Diabetes

DIABETES AFFECTS MANY areas of health and daily living. People with diabetes must take responsibility for their day-to-day care in order to keep the symptoms of diabetes under control and prevent dangerous complications. This involves a number of steps and can be very intensive. Consequently, living with diabetes can be a challenge. However, most diabetics find that when they take steps to actively manage diabetes the results are worth the effort. Their symptoms improve and complications are prevented. This helps people with diabetes feel more in charge of their lives. A patient explains: "Diabetes can become a very controlling factor in your life. I carefully manage my diabetes by monitoring my blood glucose levels, using fast acting insulin when I have to, exercising regularly, and staying on a strict diet. As a result, I feel very much in control of my life."[41]

Regulating Blood Glucose

Perhaps the greatest challenge diabetics face is regulating their blood glucose. Although medication, diet, and exercise lower blood glucose levels, in order to control diabetes and help lower the risk of developing long- and short-term complications, people with diabetes must monitor their blood glucose levels.

In nondiabetics glucose levels are automatically controlled by the pancreas and remain relatively constant. But in diabetics, blood glucose levels fluctuate considerably. Food, stress, and lack of insulin cause blood glucose to rise, while medication and exercise cause it to decrease. Since the pancreas is unable to control these fluctuations, self-monitoring takes over the role of the pancreas.

When patients self-monitor their blood glucose, they keep track of and control their glucose levels. Self-monitoring of blood glucose involves patients pricking a finger with a needlelike tool, called a lancet, and removing a drop of blood. The drop of blood is placed on a test strip, which is fed into a glucose meter that resembles a calculator. The meter chemically or electronically measures the amount of glucose in the drop of blood and reports the amount on a small digital display. This lets patients know if their

Diabetics use blood monitors like this one to read their glucose levels every day.

blood glucose is too high or too low. A patient explains: "It's almost painless. The lancet is spring-loaded. I hit the button and a tiny needle pricks my finger and takes some blood. Then the meter gives me a readout."[42]

By monitoring their blood before each meal and at bedtime, patients can measure the effect of their medication on their blood sugar and can make adjustments in their insulin dose when necessary. Many patients also test their blood glucose after eating to check the effect of certain foods on their body, and before and after exercising to ensure that their blood sugar has not fallen significantly. According to author Porter Shimer, "Monitoring is the key to mastery. Only by watching the ups and downs of blood sugar levels can you learn their patterns and gather information needed to control them."[43]

A study conducted by the National Institute of Diabetes and Digestive and Kidney Diseases examined the effect of frequent blood glucose monitoring on controlling diabetes. The results of the study showed that diabetics who tested their blood glucose four to seven times per day lowered their risk of developing retinopathy by 76 percent and kidney disease by 50 percent. According to diabetes expert Dr. Gerald Bernstein, "The disease can control the patient or the patient can control the disease, and glucose monitoring is at the very core of where the control begins."[44]

Keeping a Journal

In an effort to better recognize when and what causes their blood glucose to fluctuate, many patients record their blood glucose test results in a glucose journal. Patients record the date and time of their blood glucose test results, and the amount, and timing of their insulin dosage or oral medication. They note their emotional state and general health, and include specific details such as what type of food they ate; the type, intensity, and duration of exercise they participated in; and what effect these factors have on their blood glucose. Using this information, patients and doctors can discover what factors cause extremes in their blood glucose. A patient explains: "It's a little like being a scientist. If your blood sugar is higher or lower than you want it to be, you can usually figure out why. Maybe you ran extra hard today. Maybe your snack was bigger than usual. Maybe you've got bad cold. Maybe you got angry at your brother."[45]

Once specific foods and activities are identified as causing glucose levels to rise or fall patients can try to avoid them. In addition they can properly match the timing and type of insulin or medication they use to minimize glucose highs and lows. In this manner, people with diabetes gain more control over the disease.

Controlling Weight

One more measure people with diabetes often take to control diabetes symptoms and lower their risk of developing complications is losing weight. When people overeat, their pancreas must

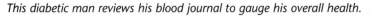

This diabetic man reviews his blood journal to gauge his overall health.

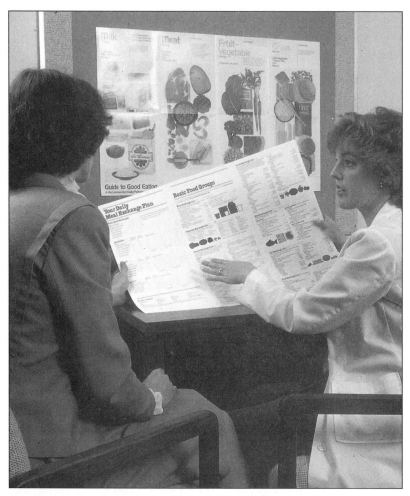

A nutritionist explains the importance of eating right to a diabetic patient.

produce extra insulin in order to maintain normal blood sugar levels. However, diabetics cannot produce sufficient insulin to balance the extra food. Thus, overeating causes blood glucose levels to rise. Moreover, being overweight can lead to dangerous complications such as heart disease, high blood pressure, and circulatory problems. According to the American Diabetes Association, a ten- to twenty-pound weight loss helps overweight diabetics control their blood sugar and reduce their risk of complications.

Losing weight is difficult for everyone, but it can be especially difficult for people with diabetes. Diabetics must maintain a balance between their glucose and insulin. To do this, they must eat often without skipping any meals. In addition, diabetics cannot substitute low calorie, high carbohydrate diet drinks for high calorie foods such as meat or dairy products. Moreover, due to exercise's effect on blood glucose, diabetics cannot increase the intensity of their workout as a way to burn excess calories unless the change is carefully monitored.

To help deal with these challenges, many people with diabetes consult a dietician to help them set up a healthy weight loss plan. A patient explains: "I've always been a bit overweight. When I was diagnosed with diabetes, my doctor told me I had to lose weight if I wanted to stay healthy. I went to a dietician who helped me plan a sensible diet that includes more fish and vegetables. I've lost eleven pounds, and I look great. But more importantly, I'm keeping myself healthy and avoiding complications."[46]

Emotional Challenges

The challenge of monitoring blood sugar, eating right, and controlling their weight causes some patients to feel that their lives center around diabetes. As a result, many patients become frustrated and depressed. Research acknowledges that people with diabetes are four times more likely to suffer from depression than nondiabetics. This may be because high blood glucose levels can make patients feel tired and unable to cope.

Depression, like stress, raises blood glucose levels. It also affects people's ability to concentrate, makes them lose interest in daily activities, increases fatigue and pain, and causes fear and anxiety. A study conducted in the University of Washington showed that diabetics who are depressed do not manage their diabetes as well as those who are not. They do not exercise, maintain a balanced diet, or test their blood glucose as frequently as they should. A doctor describes the effect of depression on a patient: "Even though she knew how to manage diabetes, she couldn't help feeling alone, helpless and down in the dumps. She just couldn't motivate herself to do what she knew she had to do."[47]

Thus, depression often worsens diabetes. In order to combat depression, many diabetics seek counseling or take antidepression medication.

Dealing with Social Situations

Even when problems with depression are solved, people with diabetes must overcome other obstacles. Maintaining control over diabetes can often be difficult in social situations. Eating in restaurants can be troublesome and embarrassing for diabetics who must check their blood glucose and inject insulin before meals. Using an insulin pen or pump helps diabetics administer insulin in public. If this is not possible, many people with diabetes test themselves and take their insulin at home. Then they dine only in restaurants where they can reserve a table for a set time, so that they are not kept waiting when they should be eating.

What is served at social events can also pose a problem for diabetics who must maintain a healthful diet and avoid sweets. This is particularly difficult for young diabetes sufferers who often attend parties where sweets are the only food served. Diabetic children solve this problem by bringing a healthy snack with them to substitute for the party food. A parent of a diabetic explains: "I remember the first school party after Cullinan [her son] was diagnosed. The other kids were eating cupcakes and Cullinan was eating hard-boiled eggs and carrots. Now I bring sugar-free candy and ice cream for everyone and all the kids love it. You make adjustments."[48]

Challenges at School

Managing diabetes at school presents other challenges for youthful diabetics. Even when students with diabetes are receiving treatment for the disease, because of the way blood glucose levels fluctuate, they may occasionally have problems with diabetes' symptoms, such as frequent urination and thirst. Consequently, they may need to leave the classroom to drink water and urinate more frequently than nondiabetics. In addition, they must eat a snack during class to prevent hypoglycemia and inject insulin and monitor blood glucose. "Diabetes and school is hard," a young diabetic explains. "Every day around 10:30 I test my blood glucose to start getting ready for lunch. While I'm in the office doing that, I miss some of my math class. During lunch I have to figure out how much insulin I need. In the days I have ski practice, I have to test around 2:00. I test again before I go on the trails and adjust my insulin or eat a snack as needed."[49]

Young diabetics must learn how to self-administer insulin within the demands of a busy schedule.

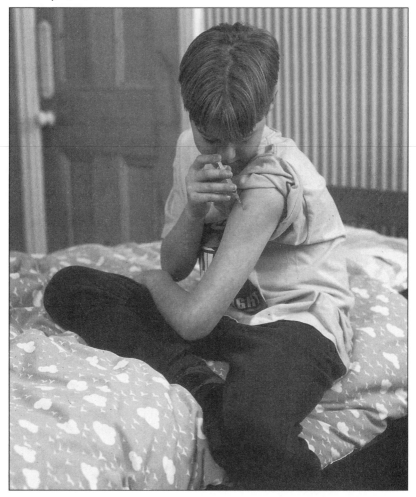

According to a survey conducted by the American Diabetes Association, 73 percent of the youthful diabetics surveyed reported problems with their schools accommodating their special needs. One way youthful diabetics overcome such problems is by developing a school action plan. This plan includes information from the student's doctor informing teachers, school officials, and the school nurse about the student's diabetes, what the symptoms are, what medications and blood tests are needed, and what procedure to follow in an emergency. Such a plan strengthens communication between patients, their doctor, and the school.

Keeping these people informed helps students with diabetes manage their diabetes at school more effectively. For example, teachers may permit diabetic students to leave the room or eat a snack whenever it is necessary, and they may monitor students more closely than usual for symptoms of hyperglycemia or hypoglycemia. Moreover, because many schools do not permit students to carry any form of medication, including insulin, with them, students have to store their insulin in the nurse's office. This can be especially dangerous when students' blood sugar levels get too high and require an immediate dose of insulin. The time wasted in walking to the nurse's office may cause the student to develop ketoacidosis. A patient explains: "My mom sometimes has to fight with some of my teachers against rules like going to the clinic for insulin. Like if a kid is having a diabetic episode [ketoacidosis] he's not going to have time to walk to the clinic."[50] However, with an action plan on file, school officials often permit students with diabetes to keep their insulin with them, allowing them to respond quickly to high blood glucose.

Feeling Different

Managing diabetes at school makes many youthful diabetics feel self-conscious and different. This can be a particular problem for teenagers who are at a stage in their lives where they are struggling to fit in with their peers. As a result, many teenagers with diabetes ignore their glucose monitoring and diets in order to be more like everyone else.

Such behavior can cause diabetic symptoms to worsen and increase the risk of complications developing in diabetics of any age. But it is especially risky in teenagers whose insulin and glucose levels fluctuate dramatically due to growth spurts and hormonal changes during puberty. A patient recalls her experience:

> It isn't easy to grow up with diabetes. My first year of high school was the worst. I hated being different. I hated having to eat healthy while everyone else was guzzling sodas and fries. I hated testing my sugar before and after basketball practice. I cheated a lot, candy bars, Cokes, fried onion rings, and I didn't test as often as I should have. Going into the hospital with ketoacidosis at fifteen was my wake-up call. That scared me enough to take action. It wasn't easy, but now I'm back in control, and my friends support my choice.[51]

Lives Changed

Both juvenile and adult diabetics find that in order to manage diabetes effectively they have to make a number of changes in their lives. Many of these changes involve what and when diabetics eat. For example, many patients find that by eating their meals at the same time every day and by eating the same foods often, they can better predict and thus control their blood glucose level. A patient explains: "I have to eat my meals on a strict schedule. That means the evening meal is ready by 4:15 daily. Also, I eat exactly the same thing for lunch and breakfast every day hoping to have enough complex carbohydrate in my system to ward off hypoglycemia."[52]

Another dietary change diabetics make is avoiding alcohol. Alcohol is a chemical that lowers blood glucose significantly, increases the effect of insulin on the body, and blocks the liver from releasing glycogen. Consequently, when diabetics drink alcohol the result is often severe hypoglycemia. This is especially dangerous when alcohol is taken without food. In addition, mixing alcohol with oral medication for diabetes can cause reactions such as nausea, headaches, and sweating.

Though smoking is hazardous to everyone's health, diabetics may suffer worse neuropathy and high blood pressure as a result.

Similarly, people with diabetes must refrain from smoking. Although smoking presents health hazards for everyone, it is especially dangerous for diabetics. Nicotine, a chemical in cigarettes, causes blood vessels to narrow, restricting blood flow throughout the body. By restricting blood flow, smoking increases a diabetic's chances of developing or worsening complications from diabetes such as neuropathy, high blood pressure, and foot wounds that will not heal. In fact, more than 90 percent of diabetics who have a limb amputated are smokers. A patient explains:

My father smoked a pack of cigarettes a day for thirty years. When he was diagnosed with diabetes he stopped smoking. But the damage was already done. By the time he was sixty, he had almost no circulation in his feet. He was plagued with foot ulcers [wounds in the feet that will not heal], and could barely walk. The only thing the doctor could do was amputate his leg. It was all caused by smoking combined with diabetes.[53]

Avoiding Complications

In addition to making changes in their lives, it is important that diabetics maintain good health practices in order to prevent complications from developing. This includes attentive foot care. Because of poor circulation and neuropathy, people with diabetes may be unaware of small cuts or bruises on their feet. When left untreated, those wounds can lead to infection and amputation. Diabetics reduce or eliminate the threat of infection and amputation by washing and inspecting their feet daily. This includes checking for cracks and cuts and treating even minor injuries with antiseptic. In addition, to avoid dry skin, which can lead to the skin cracking, many diabetics massage their feet daily with a special cream that contains a moisturizing substance called lanolin. Massaging helps improve circulation, and lanolin helps prevent the skin from cracking. A patient explains: "I examine my feet every night before bed. I check for bruises and scratches, and I rub them with a cream my doctor gave me."[54]

People with diabetes also must practice good eye care to avoid blindness caused by diabetes. This includes checking their own vision weekly to look for any changes such as blurriness, fuzzy areas, or red spots, which may indicate the development of retinopathy, and having an eye doctor examine their eyes once a year. If problems are discovered early, they can be corrected and blindness can usually be prevented. A patient explains: "I noticed that things were starting to look blurry, and I sometimes saw a dark spot. I went right to the eye doctor. He checked my eyes and gave me some medicine. He told me to keep watching my vision. That way, with the doctor's help, hopefully, I can prevent any serious problems."[55]

Being Prepared

Because diabetic emergencies can occur even when people with diabetes manage diabetes carefully, diabetics protect themselves by being prepared to cope with emergencies. This involves carrying diabetic supplies such as medicine, insulin, syringes, and a glucose monitor whenever diabetics plan to be away from home. Diabetics must also carry candy or glucose tablets with them at all times. Because candy and glucose tablets are simple carbohydrates that are immediately turned into glucose by the body, they raise blood sugar quickly when hypoglycemia threatens.

Many diabetics also wear a special bracelet or necklace that identifies them as a diabetic. This provides information to others

Worn responsibly, these medical bracelets identify the wearer as diabetic and are helpful in emergencies.

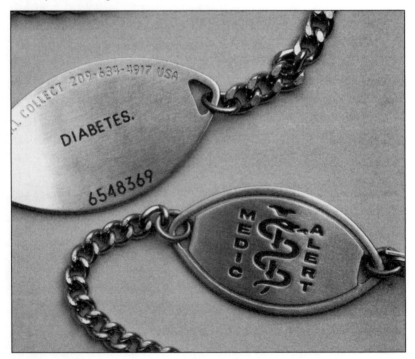

in case of diabetic emergencies such as hypoglycemia. Because hypoglycemia often makes it difficult for diabetics to think clearly, sufferers may not be able to supply health information in an emergency. Due to their strange behavior, diabetics suffering from hypoglycemia may be mistaken for substance abusers. A diabetic identification bracelet helps police to distinguish between these two problems and to provide diabetics with the help they need. Dr. Alan L. Rubin describes a patient's experience: "One of my patients was driving on a highway when another driver noticed that she was weaving back and forth and reported her to the highway patrol. A patrolman stopped her, concluded that she was drunk, and took her to jail. Fortunately, someone noticed that she was wearing a diabetes medical bracelet. After promptly receiving the nutrition she needed, she rapidly recovered."[56]

Support Groups

Although living with diabetes can be challenging, diabetics use a number of strategies to help them cope and enjoy their lives. Among these strategies is participating in support groups. Diabetes support groups are made up of diabetics who share their experiences. These groups give members a chance to share their feelings and provide information, encouragement, and a sense of belonging. By sharing their common experiences, support group members often find solutions to problems that nondiabetics do not understand. A patient who attends a support group explains how it has helped her: "We started out with about 15 folks. And did we have a lot to say to each other! We talked about food. We also discussed what it was like being a diabetic in the real world. We struggled with the same problems, but seeing the way different people solve problems opened up a world of possibilities."[57]

There are diabetes support groups all over the country for diabetics of all ages. Organizations such as the American Diabetes Association sponsor local support groups in towns and cities all over the United States. In addition, there are electronic support groups that share information via the Internet.

A young girl tests her blood glucose levels at a camp specially designed for young diabetics.

Camps

Many children and young adults with diabetes also learn how to cope with their disease by spending their summers attending special camps sponsored by the American Diabetes Association. By teaching youthful diabetics how to monitor their glucose and inject insulin, and how to deal with high and low blood glucose, diabetes camps help juvenile patients learn ways to meet the challenges they face every day.

Diabetes camps provide a safe environment for young diabetics. Campers share healthy meals that follow a strict diabetic diet. The camps also give children with diabetes a chance to participate in physical activities like white-water rafting, swimming, and softball, allowing them to have fun with other children and young adults like themselves. And all activities are supervised by special medical staff, trained in the care of diabetes. A camper explains: "Camp was awesome. I learned how to test my blood and take shots at camp. The food is healthy, so I never had to worry about it. All the kids at camp have the same experiences, so I never felt different. Going there made having diabetes easier."[58]

By combining the skills patients learn in support groups and diabetes camp with careful daily care and lifestyle changes, people with diabetes gain control over their symptoms and decrease their chances of developing dangerous complications. "I am fortunate that diabetes is something I can control," a patient explains. "If I take care of myself, I can lead a healthy life."[59]

Chapter 5

What the Future Holds

ALTHOUGH PEOPLE WHO actively manage diabetes lead productive lives, diabetes and its complications result in the deaths of about 450,000 Americans each year, and new cases continue to increase. Consequently, most diabetes research is focused on investigating ways to prevent or delay the development of the disease. And, because managing diabetes is so intensive, researchers are also developing easier and more effective forms of treatment.

Blame It on Modern Life

In spite of the fact that people have been afflicted with diabetes for hundreds of years, new cases of diabetes have more than tripled during the last forty years. The greatest increase has been in rich, industrialized countries while the number of cases has remained stable in more primitive rural communities. Therefore, scientists think that lifestyle changes have stimulated this surge in diabetes cases. By analyzing how life in modern communities differs from life in primitive communities, researchers are trying to pinpoint specific lifestyle changes that have fueled the increase in diabetes rates.

Scientists have identified two main lifestyle changes common to people in prosperous nations. The first is the availability of food. This, experts think, has resulted in people overeating and becoming overweight, which causes their pancreases to work harder than normal. The second is a decline in physical activity, which causes people's blood glucose levels to rise. Scientists theorize that these two changes have fueled the increase in diabetes rates.

By comparing the incidence of diabetes in prosperous industrial populations to those in more primitive rural environments, scientists are gaining evidence to support their theory. In 2002 Dr. Mehmood Khan, an expert at the Mayo Clinic, examined the incidence of diabetes among Somali immigrants moving from poor rural villages in Africa to the United States. Dr. Khan found dramatic increases in diabetes rates among immigrant families. According to Dr. Khan, "In their homeland, Somalis walk and ride bikes, have far fewer labor-saving appliances and eat food containing little fat. But once they reach America, their physical activity drops precipitously and their diet shifts toward American diets. Something happens. The question is, what is it?"[60]

Dietary Changes

In order to pinpoint exactly what is happening, scientists are examining what dietary changes have taken place. Many scientists speculate that overeating and the weight gain it causes, combined with the popularity of high fat, processed foods, which are absorbed into the bloodstream rapidly, are linked to the increase in the incidence of diabetes.

By comparing the diet and incidence of diabetes in high-risk groups, with that of their ancestors, scientists are investigating this link. For example, statistics show that there were no known cases of diabetes among Native Americans before 1936. However, by 2000 as many as 50 percent of all members of some tribes, such as the Pima Indians, developed diabetes.

In the past, Native Americans ate more traditional foods such as fresh fruits, vegetables, meat, and fish, and their daily activities included gardening, hunting, and fishing. Due to changes in society, most Native Americans have adopted an inactive lifestyle and diets rich in processed foods. These changes, scientists speculate, encourage diabetes to develop. At the 2001 National Diabetes Conference, Elizabeth Gaines-Gray, the conference coordinator, explained: "The Indian people had wisdom in what they ate. The issue is that traditional foods are more healthy than westernized refined carbohydrates. Those foods are totally stripped of nutrients."[61]

In an effort to compare the effects of a modern diet to a traditional diet, the National Institute of Diabetes and Digestive and Kidney Diseases has been monitoring the diet and activity level of Pima Indian volunteers for more than thirty years. During this time, the volunteers who ate a healthier diet and were more physically active had a lower incidence of diabetes than those who were more sedentary and ate a modern diet. According to researcher Dr. Bill Knowler, "Thirty years of research show that exercising and eating lower fat, fiber-rich foods can at least delay diabetes. If you delay it long enough, it's almost as good as preventing it."[62]

Based on the success of the Pima Indian study, the National Institutes of Health launched a similar, nationwide study, known as the Diabetes Prevention Program, in the hopes of preventing or delaying the development of diabetes in Native Americans.

A Pima Indian man exercises on a treadmill to help manage his diabetes.

Scientists predict that if Native Americans consume a healthier, more traditional diet and assume a more active lifestyle their risk of developing diabetes will decrease significantly. In order to accomplish this, subjects from several Indian tribes modified their eating habits and increased their physical activity. Early results from the study are promising. Most participants lowered their blood glucose levels significantly, thus delaying the onset of diabetes. According to researcher Dr. Christopher D. Saudek, "The DPP [Diabetes Prevention Program] is one of the most important studies in the recent history of diabetes. It conclusively proves that type 2 diabetes is not inevitable for people at high risk of developing it."[63] Based on the study's success, scientists hope to prescribe similar diet and lifestyle changes to other high-risk groups such as African Americans and Hispanics.

Identifying Nutrients

In an effort to identify specific nutrients that may delay the development of diabetes, researchers are closely examining particular foods commonly eaten in the past and comparing them to foods commonly eaten today. In doing this, scientists have determined that daily consumption of fruits and vegetables has diminished significantly. Researchers at the University of California at Los Angeles found that early humans ate at least twelve servings of vegetables and fruit each day. In contrast, according to the American Dietetic Association, 11 percent of modern Americans eat no daily servings of fruits or vegetables. And, although the U.S. Department of Agriculture's food pyramid recommends that people eat at least five servings of fruits and vegetables each day, only about 9 percent of Americans observe this recommendation.

Since vegetables and fruit are a rich source of essential vitamins and minerals, antioxidants, and dietary fiber, scientists believe that their decreased consumption may be linked to deficiencies in valuable nutrients. And this may be associated with the development of diabetes. Among the nutrients that scientists are investigating are fiber, allylpropyl-disulfide, quercetin, and vitamin B complex.

Fiber

Fruits and vegetables provide the body with fiber. Evidence from a number of studies shows that people who consume a high-fiber diet have lower blood sugar than those who do not. Scientists think that this is because fiber is bulky. Consequently, fibrous foods are gradually absorbed into the bloodstream, slowing down digestion and the normal blood sugar increase after eating. To test the effect of a diet rich in fiber on people with diabetes, a study at the University of Texas Southwestern Medical Center in 2000 had a group of diabetics eat seven to eight servings of fruits and vegetables each day for six weeks. At the end of the six weeks the subjects' blood glucose was checked. All of the subjects in the group had lowered their blood glucose levels by at least 10 percent. According to researcher Dr. James W. Anderson, "Fiber appears to slow the passage of glucose from food into the cells. As a result, less insulin is needed to control blood sugar."[64]

Although all fruits and vegetables are good sources of fiber, scientists also have been studying the effects of legumes such as green beans, pinto beans, and red beans on blood glucose. Scientists have focused on legumes because they are especially high in fiber and were an important component of the traditional diet of both Native Americans and Hispanics.

Results of a number of studies show that legumes appear to help control blood sugar. Research in Canada, for example, monitored the blood glucose levels of men who ate beans and those who did not. The subjects who ate the most beans had the lowest blood glucose levels and were the least likely to develop diabetes. Consequently, scientists theorize that a diet rich in fiber, and especially beans, may have a role in preventing or delaying diabetes. A patient who has added legumes to her diet explains: "My doctor suggested that I eat beans once a day to help control my blood sugar. I have a cup of white beans every night. My blood sugar has dropped almost twenty points since I started. I've told my children to eat more beans too. They don't have diabetes yet. Maybe eating beans can keep them from getting it."[65]

Consuming high-fiber fruits and vegetables is one way to lower blood sugar levels.

Garlic and Onions

Allylpropyl-disulfide is another nutrient researchers think lowers blood glucose and when eaten often may delay the onset of diabetes. Allylpropyl-disulfide is a flavonoid, a nutrient responsible for the color of a fruit or vegetable. It is found in garlic, which has been used as a folk remedy to treat illnesses such as diabetes and heart disease for hundreds of years.

There is mounting evidence that garlic does have a number of medicinal benefits. It has been found to be an antioxidant and a

Scientists speculate that eating onions and garlic increases insulin production and lowers blood sugar.

natural antibiotic. In addition, although scientists are unsure why, it has been shown to significantly lower blood glucose. Scientists speculate that some unknown property of the allylpropyl-disulfide in garlic stimulates insulin production. In an ongoing study reported by the *Lawrence Review of Natural Products*, an alternative treatment journal, garlic has been shown to increase insulin in the blood, improve the liver's ability to store and use glycogen, and reduce blood sugar in both humans and animals.

Like allylpropyl-disulfide, quercetin, a flavonoid found in onions, also appears to lower blood glucose. In addition, quercetin appears to help prevent diabetic retinopathy by blocking blood sugar from accumulating in and narrowing the blood vessels in the eyes. Scientists are unsure why quercetin has this effect, but they theorize that an unknown chemical in quercetin stimulates the pancreas to produce insulin. Research has shown that people who check their blood glucose, then eat onions and recheck their blood glucose, have lower blood sugar after eating onions. The more onions the subjects eat, the more their blood glucose levels decrease.

Although research on allylpropyl-disulfide and quercetin is still preliminary, the results are encouraging, and research is continuing. As a result, many people with diabetes and others at risk of developing the disease are adding more garlic and onions to their diet. Diabetes expert Porter Shimer explains: "Onions and garlic contain substances that appear to slow the rise of blood sugar. Given the safety of these foods, it certainly couldn't hurt to incorporate them whenever possible into meals."[66]

Vitamin B Complex

Vitamin B complex is another nutrient found in fruits and vegetables. Many experts believe that this group of B vitamins plays an important role in preventing diabetes. Although experts are unsure why, vitamin B complex, which includes vitamins B_1, B_2, B_3, B_6, B_{12}, inositol, and biotin, appear to help the body digest carbohydrates and use glucose effectively. Scientists believe that deficiencies of these vitamins may play a part in the development of diabetes. For instance, research has shown that 3 percent of people with diabetes are deficient in vitamin B_{12}, and many people with type I diabetes have low blood levels of vitamin B_1. Other studies have found that people with low levels of vitamin B_6 often are unable to produce adequate insulin.

In addition, because B vitamins are antioxidants, they help block glucose from building up in nerve cells, thus protecting diabetics from developing diabetic neuropathy. In fact, a number of studies have found that patients with neuropathy often are deficient in one or more B vitamins. Consequently, researchers are examining the effects of supplementing the diet of diabetic subjects with B vitamins in an effort to stop or delay the development of diabetic neuropathy. A 1997 study in Africa found that treating diabetes patients with vitamins B_1 and B_6 reduced symptoms of diabetic neuropathy by 50 percent. Another study

Found naturally in fruits and vegetables, vitamin B reduces the incidence of diabetic neuropathy.

conducted in the University of Alabama in 1999 also found a significant improvement in nerve functions of diabetics who were fed a diet rich in inositol. Therefore, many experts are encouraging diabetics to eat foods rich in B vitamins because of their many health benefits. These foods include citrus fruit, mushrooms, bananas, and green vegetables.

Even though scientists have not found conclusive evidence that eating foods abundant in fiber, allylpropyl-disulfide, quercetin, and B vitamins can prevent diabetes, it appears that eating a healthy diet can reduce blood glucose and delay the onset of diabetic complications. Researcher Dr. Jaako Tuomilehto says: "This should be very encouraging news for people at high risk for developing diabetes."[67]

Genetic Factors

While researchers are investigating the role nutrients play, other scientists are looking even deeper into the body at the role genes play in the development of diabetes. Genes are found in the cells of every living thing and determine individual traits such as hair color, eye color, and height. They are passed down from parents to children. Because diabetes commonly runs in families, scientists think that the tendency to develop the disease is inherited.

Therefore, researchers are trying to find specific genes shared by diabetes patients that may encourage the development of diabetes. Once these genes are identified, scientists hope to develop ways to change or replace these genes in order to prevent diabetes from developing. To accomplish this a number of groups including the National Institutes of Health and the American Diabetes Association are developing family trees and gathering DNA, the chemicals that determine an organism's genetic makeup, from blood samples of diabetic volunteers and their family members. By comparing and analyzing the DNA of different family members, researchers hope to identify different genes that may be involved in causing diabetes.

Among these studies is an ongoing study of Pima Indians, whom scientists have been tracking for several years. Since 1983 scientists have been studying DNA samples of 90 percent of Pima tribe members. By comparing the DNA of Pima Indians who have diabetes to those who do not, scientists seek to pinpoint

A home health nurse assists a diabetic Pima Indian woman; scientists are trying to determine why the Pima are genetically more susceptible to diabetes.

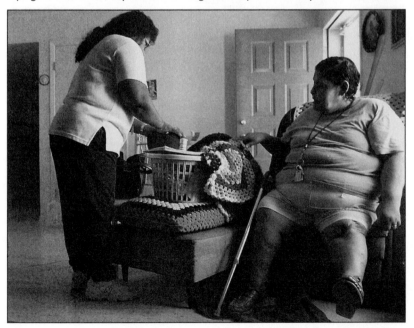

specific mutated genes shared by the subjects with diabetes. One such gene, called *FABP2*, was found in diabetic Pima subjects, but not in nondiabetic subjects. Experts think this gene causes the body to break down fats more rapidly than normal. This causes blood glucose levels to rise. However, since the pancreas works best when fat is broken down slowly, insulin production does not rise as well.

Scientists also suspect that diabetics may have other mutant genes that inhibit or interfere with beta cells' ability to produce insulin. Through continuing studies of Pima Indian volunteers, researchers hope to identify these genes. Once these genes are identified, scientists will be better able to predict who will develop diabetes and take steps to delay or prevent its development. Researcher Dr. Bill Knowler explains: "If we can locate the genes contributing to the disease, we can identify which people are at high risk for the disease and figure out ways to intervene."[68]

Prediabetes

One way scientists are already intervening is by identifying people with a family history of diabetes and screening them for a condition known as prediabetes. Patients with prediabetes have between 110 and 125 blood glucose levels on a fasting glucose test. This is higher than normal, but not yet diabetic. Studies have shown that most people with this condition develop diabetes within ten years.

Consequently, a number of groups, including the National Institutes of Health, are conducting continuing studies in which prediabetics are being treated with diet and lifestyle changes, and with the drug metformin, in an effort to delay or prevent the development of diabetes. So far, the results have been excellent. Fifty-eight percent of the subjects studied lowered their risk of developing diabetes through dietary changes and exercise, and 31 percent reduced their risk of developing diabetes through treatment with metformin. Therefore, doctors are being urged to closely screen people who may have prediabetes. U.S. secretary of Health and Human Services, Tommy G. Thompson, explains: "The good news is if you have pre-diabetes, you can do something about it. We want people to know that pre-diabetes is a serious condition that can be reversed or alleviated with modest changes in their daily routine."[69]

Improving Treatment

While some scientists are working hard to discover ways to prevent diabetes from striking new patients, others are developing new and easier forms of treatment in an effort to make managing diabetes easier. Since most diabetics would prefer to avoid insulin injections, researchers are testing a number of alternative insulin delivery devices that they hope diabetics could use in place of injections.

One such device is sprayable insulin. Like sore throat spray, sprayable insulin is absorbed into the bloodstream when subjects spray it into their throats. Currently being developed by a pharmaceutical company, sprayable insulin appears to be as effective as injected rapid-acting insulin. In a test on eleven subjects, sprayable insulin outperformed rapid-acting insulin in its rate of absorption into the bloodstream and its glucose lowering ability. Tests are continuing, and researchers hope that sprayable insulin will be available to the public within the next five years.

Scientists also are working on developing an insulin patch that works like a nicotine patch. Such a patch slowly releases insulin through the skin into the bloodstream. So far, animal tests have been successful. But, because of the shape of insulin molecules, only a fraction of the insulin on the patch is able to penetrate human skin, and the patch has caused skin problems in some of the subjects. However, scientists hope to develop an effective insulin patch in the future.

Other researchers have been trying to create an insulin pill for more than seventy years. They have had little success because digestive juices in the stomach destroy insulin that is taken orally before it can be used by the body. Nonetheless, researchers at Purdue University in Indiana have recently created a plastic coating for an insulin pill that keeps digestive juices from destroying the insulin. So far, animal tests have been promising. But, experts predict it will be some time before such a pill will be available for humans. However with the number of noninvasive insulin delivery devices being studied, researchers are confident that it will not be long before diabetics will no longer have to use needles. Researcher Alessio Fasano predicts, "The future for people with diabetes will be one without needles."[70]

Implantable Insulin Pumps

Scientists are also investigating ways to make using an insulin pump easier. Rather than patients wearing an external insulin pump, scientists are developing an insulin pump that can be directly implanted inside the patient's abdomen. This pump, which is about the size of a hockey puck, can deliver insulin effectively for about four years. About eight hundred pumps have been implanted successfully in test subjects in the last twenty years. However, since the tube carrying the insulin can become obstructed, researchers are still working on perfecting the device before making it available to the public.

Noninvasive Glucose Meter

Over the years, scientists have been trying to develop a noninvasive glucose meter. Such a meter could check patients' blood glucose levels without puncturing their skin. This has been difficult since glucose monitoring requires a blood sample. However, in March 2001 the U.S. government approved a noninvasive glucose meter, known as the Gluco Watch Biographer, for use by diabetics. The Gluco Watch Biographer looks like a wristwatch. It is worn on the wrist and has a small patch on the underside, which is attached to the wearer's skin. Using a small electric current, it painlessly draws glucose through the patch. The glucose is then measured by electrons and is reported every twenty minutes on the watch face. Similar devices that use electrons and a patch but are worn on other parts of the body are currently in development, as are glucose monitoring devices that use painless lasers rather than a lancet to gather blood samples.

With the development of new noninvasive insulin delivery systems and blood glucose monitoring devices, researchers are

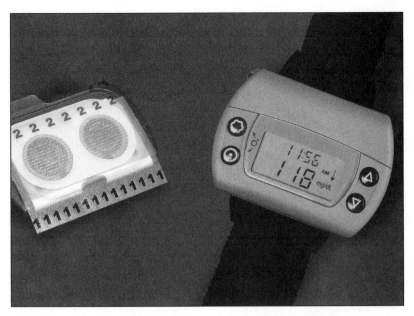

While other glucose meters require a lancet to draw blood, the noninvasive Gluco Watch Biographer measures glucose levels electronically.

helping to make managing diabetes easier. At the same time, by identifying factors that encourage diabetes to develop, researchers hope to prevent new cases of diabetes and prevent people with diabetes from developing dangerous complications. As a result, the future looks bright for people with diabetes. As Dr. Christopher D. Saudek reports in the *Journal of the American Medical Association*, "Opportunities for progress are virtually limitless."[71]

Notes

Introduction: A Developing Epidemic

1. Chelsea, personal interview with author, Dallas, TX, July 8, 2002.
2. Quoted in *Lifescan.com*, "Diabetes Growing Fastest in Asia." www.lifescan.com.
3. Quoted in *Diabetic-Lifestyle.com*, "The Diabetes Epidemic." www.diabetic-lifestyle.com.
4. Chelsea, personal interview with author.
5. Chelsea, personal interview with author.

Chapter 1: What Is Diabetes?

6. Quoted in *Children with Diabetes*, "Winning with Diabetes." www.childrenwithdiabetes.com.
7. Quoted in *Children with Diabetes*, "Andrew." www.childrenwithdiabetes.com.
8. Alan L. Rubin, *Diabetes for Dummies*. New York: Hungry Minds, 1999, p. 34.
9. Ingrid, personal interview with author, Dallas, TX, June 18, 2002.
10. Chris Kuell, "Tips for the Newly Blind Diabetic," *Voice of the Diabetic*, vol. 14, no. 3, Summer 1999. www.nfb.org.
11. Quoted in *Kidney Directions*, "Diabetes Management." www.kidneydirections.com.
12. Neil M. Scheffler, "One Step Ahead of Amputation," *American Diabetes Association*. www.diabetes.org.
13. Quoted in Terri D'Arrigo, "Ketoacidosis: The Snake in the Grass," *Diabetes Forecast*, July 2001, p. 70.

Chapter 2: Diagnosis and Treatment

14. Quoted in *Children with Diabetes*, "Norm L. Hefner." www.childrenwithdiabetes.com.
15. *Children with Diabetes*, "Injected with Life." www.childrenwithdiabetes.com.
16. Marilyn, personal interview with author, New York, NY, June 7, 2002.
17. Quoted in Rubin, *Diabetes for Dummies*, p. 23.
18. Steve, personal interview with author, Las Cruces, NM, June 28, 2002.
19. Quoted in *Children with Diabetes*, "Joshua Halberg." www.childrenwithdiabetes.com.
20. Quoted in Terri D'Arrigo, "Best-Kept Secret or Simply a Gadget?" *American Diabetes Association*. www.diabetes.org.
21. Quoted in Kate McClare, "Destructive Disease," *Boca Raton News*, November 24, 1999.
22. Damaso, personal interview with author, San Antonio, TX, June 4, 2002.
23. Sue K. Milchovich and Barbara Dunn-Long, *Diabetes Mellitus*. Palo Alto, CA: Bull Publishing, 1999, p. 22.
24. Quoted in Porter Shimer, *New Hope for People with Diabetes*. Roseville, CA: Prima, 2001, p. 126.
25. Rick, personal interview with author, Dallas,TX, May 7, 2002.
26. Rick, personal interview with author.
27. Quoted in Shimer, *New Hope for People with Diabetes*, p. 171.
28. Shimer, *New Hope for People with Diabetes*, p. 171.
29. Quoted in Shimer, *New Hope for People with Diabetes*, p. 172.

Chapter 3: Alternative and Complementary Treatment

30. Quoted in David Drum, *Alternative Therapies for Managing Diabetes*. Chicago: McGraw Hill, 2002, p. 3.
31. Quoted in Drum, *Alternative Therapies for Managing Diabetes*, p. 23.
32. Quoted in *CNN.com*, "Atkins' Diet: Can We Have Our Turkey and Eat It Too?" *Crossfire*, November 26, 1999. www.cnn.com.
33. Quoted in Drum, *Alternative Therapies for Managing Diabetes*, p. 57.

34. Marilyn, personal interview with author.
35. Drum, *Alternative Therapies for Managing Diabetes*, p. 141.
36. Bea, personal interview with author, Dallas, TX, July 1, 2002.
37. Bea, personal interview with author.
38. Quoted in Drum, *Alternative Therapies for Managing Diabetes*, p. 210.
39. Quoted in Holly Firfer, "Herbal Remedies Unproven as Diabetes Treatments," *diabetic-help.com*. www.diabetic-help.com.
40. Bea, personal interview with author.

Chapter 4: Living with Diabetes

41. Steve, personal interview with author.
42. Rick, personal interview with author.
43. Shimer, *New Hope for People with Diabetes*, p. 95.
44. Quoted in Shimer, *New Hope for People with Diabetes*, p. 100.
45. Quoted in Ernest Lowe and Gary Arsham, *Diabetes: A Guide to Living Well*. Minneapolis, MN: Chronimed, 1997, p. 322.
46. Bea, personal interview with author.
47. Quoted in *American Diabetes Association Complete Guide to Diabetes*.
    Alexandria, VA: American Diabetes Association, 1999, p. 362.
48. Quoted in Marcia Levine Mazur and Carlea Bauman, "Cullinan's World," *Diabetes Forecast*, May 2002, p. 61.
49. Quoted in *Enchanted Kingdom*, "Daily Life with Diabetes." http://members.tripod.com.
50. Quoted in Kate McClare, "Destructive Disease," *Boca Raton News Online*. www.bocaratonnews.com
51. Chelsea, personal interview with author.
52. Steve, personal interview with author.
53. Bea, personal interview with author.
54. Marilyn, personal interview with author.
55. Marilyn, personal interview with author.
56. Rubin, *Diabetes for Dummies*, p. 48.
57. Quoted in Lowe and Arsham, *Diabetes: A Guide to Living Well*, p. 129.
58. Chelsea, personal interview with author.
59. Quoted in *Children with Diabetes*, "Kelli's Page." www.childrenwithdiabetes.com.

Chapter 5: What the Future Holds

60. Quoted in Tom Majeski, "Diabetes Is on Rise Among U.S. Somalis," *Diabetes Newswire.* www.twincities.com.
61. Quoted in Rick Mendosa, "Native American Diabetes," *American Diabetes Association.* www.diabetes.org.
62. Quoted in *National Institute of Diabetes and Digestive and Kidney Disorders*, "The Pima Indians Pathfinders for Health." www.niddk.nih.gov.
63. Quoted in *American Diabetes Association*, "Diabetes Prevention Program Yields Success." www.diabetes.org.
64. Quoted in Shimer, *New Hope for People with Diabetes*, p. 142.
65. Marilyn, personal interview with author.
66. Shimer, *New Hope for People with Diabetes*, p. 227.
67. Quoted in Shimer, *New Hope for People with Diabetes*, p. 160.
68. Quoted in "The Pima Indians Pathfinders for Health."
69. Quoted in *American Diabetes Association*, "Pre-Diabetes Affects Millions." www.diabetes.org.
70. Quoted in Shimer, *New Hope for People with Diabetes*, p. 277.
71. Christopher D. Saudek, "Progress and Promise of Diabetes Research," *JAMA.* www.jama.ama-assn.org.

Glossary

allylpropyl-disulfide: A nutrient found in garlic that researchers think may lower blood glucose.

antioxidants: Substances that strengthen the body by fighting against free radicals.

autoimmune disease: A disease in which the immune system attacks cells in the body.

beta cells: Cells in the pancreas that produce insulin.

chelation therapy: An alternative treatment for circulatory problems caused by diabetes.

chronic disease: A disease without a cure that afflicts sufferers for life.

complications of diabetes: Medical problems throughout the body caused by diabetes.

dehydroepiandrosterone (DHEA): A hormone used as an alternative treatment for diabetes.

diabetes: A disease in which the body produces insufficient insulin.

diabetic: A person who has diabetes.

diabetic neuropathy: Complications in the nervous system caused by diabetes.

dimethyl sulfoxide (DMSO): A powerful chemical in paint thinner used as an alternative treatment for diabetic neuropathy.

fasting glucose plasma test: A blood test used to diagnose diabetes that measures the level of glucose in the blood after a patient has fasted for eight to twelve hours.

flavonoid: A nutrient that gives fruits and vegetables their color.

free radicals: Chemicals that weaken the body and cause disease.

glitazone: An oral medication for type II diabetes.

glucose: A form of simple sugar that is the body's primary source of fuel.

glycogen: Extra glucose that is stored in the liver.

hormone: A chemical produced by the body.

hyperglycemia: A condition in which blood sugar levels are dangerously high.

hypoglycemia: A condition in which blood sugar levels are dangerously low.

insulin: A hormone that enables glucose to enter cells.

insulin pen: A device for delivering insulin into the body that resembles a ballpoint pen.

insulin pump: A small device that delivers a steady slow stream of insulin into patients.

jet injector: An insulin delivery tool that sends a premeasured dose of insulin directly into the patient through the use of a high pressure air mechanism that acts like a liquid needle.

ketoacidosis: A short-term complication of diabetes caused by the break down of fat for energy.

ketones: A dangerous by-product of the break down of fat for energy in the body.

metaformin: An oral medication for type II diabetes.

pancreas: An organ located between the stomach and the liver whose main job is producing and controlling the body's use of insulin.

quercetin: A nutrient found in onions that is believed to lower blood glucose.

random glucose plasma test: A blood test used to diagnose diabetes that measures the level of glucose in the blood.

retinopathy: Problems in the eyes caused by diabetes.

sulfonylurea: An oral medication for type II diabetes.

type I diabetes: An autoimmune disease in which the body loses its ability to produce insulin.

type II diabetes: A type of diabetes in which the pancreas produces insulin, but the body responds to it in an abnormal way.

Organizations to Contact

The following organizations may be contacted to learn more about diabetes.

American Diabetes Association
1701 North Beauregard Street
Alexandria, VA 22311
(800) 342-2383
(703) 549-1500
website: www.diabetes.org

The American Diabetes Association provides support, information, and funds for diabetes research. It offers a large variety of free information, a magazine, *Diabetes Forecast*, online diabetes links, and sponsors diabetes camps and support groups nationwide. There are many local chapters.

American Dietetic Association
216 W. Jackson Boulevard, #800
Chicago, IL 60606
(800) 366-1655
website: www.eatright.org

This association supplies information about dietary research. It also provides support and information to help people with diabetes assess and modify their diet.

Joslin Diabetes Foundation
1 Joslin Plaza
Boston, MA 02215
(617) 732-2440
website: www.joslin.org

This organization provides information and literature about diabetes. The Joslin Clinic supports diabetes research and provides medical care for people with diabetes.

Juvenile Diabetes Research Foundation International

120 Wall Street, 19TH Floor
New York, NY 10005
(800) 533-2875
(212) 785-9500
website: www.jdf.org

The Juvenile Diabetes Research Foundation International supports type I diabetes research. It also supplies support and information to juvenile diabetes patients and their families, and publishes a newsletter.

National Diabetes Information Clearinghouse

1 Information Way
Bethesda, MD 20892-3560
(800) 860-8747
(301) 654-3327
e-mail: ndic@info.niddk.nih.gov

The clearinghouse provides information about diabetes to people with diabetes, their families, doctors, and other health care professionals. It offers free publications and answers questions.

For Further Reading

Books

American Diabetes Association's Diabetes Cookbook. Alexandria, VA: American Diabetes Association, 2000. This book shows the reader how to plan menus appropriate for people with diabetes and includes one hundred recipes.

Alicia McAuliffe, *Growing Up with Diabetes: What Children Want Their Parents to Know.* New York: John Wiley & Sons, 1998. The author, who was diagnosed with diabetes when she was eleven years old, discusses what it is like to have diabetes and the problems diabetic children and teens face, based on her own experiences.

Carole McCormick Semple, *Diabetes.* Parsippany, NJ: Crestwood House, 1996. An easy-to-read young-adult book that talks about the history of diabetes, the discovery of insulin, what diabetes is, and what complications can arise.

Gill Stewart, *Diabetes.* San Diego, CA: Lucent Books, 1999. An informative young-adult book that discusses the history, causes, symptoms, treatment, emergencies, and complications of diabetes.

Websites

American Diabetes Association (www.diabetes.org). This association has information on every aspect of diabetes. It also sponsors research, diabetes summer camps, and has many helpful links.

Children with Diabetes (www.childrenwithdiabetes.com). This website deals with all aspects of diabetes in children and young adults. It provides online chats, research news, a store, and an online support community. It sponsors conferences and diabetes summer camps. It also offers scholarships to diabetes camps.

Diabetes and You (www.geocities.com). This website provides a number of true stories written by diabetics, links to other sites, and information about insulin reactions.

Diabetes Exercise & Sport (www.diabetes-exercise.org). This organization, also known as DESA, seeks to improve the lives of diabetics through exercise. It offers information on diet and exercise, a newsletter, and basketball camps for young people with diabetes.

Diabetes Gourmet Magazine (www.diabeticgourmet.com). This online magazine offers information about diabetes and healthy recipes especially tailored to help regulate blood glucose levels.

Diabetic Help (www.diabetic-help.com). This website is available in both English and Spanish. It provides information on diabetes and alternative treatments.

Kids R Pumping (http://member.aol.com). People share their experiences with insulin pumps on this website.

National Institute of Diabetes and Digestive and Kidney Diseases (www.niddk.nih.gov). Part of the National Institutes of Health, this institute provides health information and educational programs, sponsors diabetic research, and helps connect patients to clinical trials.

Native American Diabetes Initiative (www.nativeheritage.net). This website provides Native Americans and other interested people information about diabetes and how to manage it through a healthy lifestyle.

Rick Mendosa's Diabetes Directory (www.mendosa.com). This website sponsored by health writer Rick Mendosa offers links to fifteen pages of online resources on diabetes including articles written by the author.

What You Need to Know About Diabetes (www.diabetes. about.com). This website provides news, facts, recipes, support groups, and a subject library on diabetes. It is also available in Spanish.

Works Consulted

Books

American Diabetes Association Complete Guide to Diabetes. Alexandria, VA: American Diabetes Association, 1999. This book from the American Diabetes Association explains every aspect of diabetes and how to manage it.

David Drum, *Alternative Therapies for Managing Diabetes.* Chicago: McGraw Hill, 2002. This book details a wide variety of alternative treatment options. It explains how each treatment works, its value in treating diabetes, and possible health risks.

Ernest Lowe and Gary Arsham, *Diabetes: A Guide to Living Well.* Minneapolis, MN: Chronimed, 1997. The focus is on living with diabetes with information and strategies on how to best manage the disease.

Sue K. Milchovich and Barbara Dunn-Long, *Diabetes Mellitus.* Palo Alto, CA: Bull Publishing, 1999. This book provides information on every aspect of diabetes.

Alan L. Rubin, *Diabetes for Dummies.* New York: Hungry Minds, 1999. An easy-to-read reference book that discusses the causes, symptoms, treatment, complications, and ways of managing diabetes. It also offers a minicookbook with diabetes healthy recipes.

Porter Shimer, *New Hope for People with Diabetes.* Roseville, CA: Prima, 2001. An informative book with a wealth of information on glucose monitoring and insulin delivery systems.

103

Periodicals

Terri D'Arrigo, "Ketoacidosis: The Snake in the Grass," *Diabetes Forecast*, July 2001.

Marcia Levine Mazur and Carlea Bauman, "Cullinan's World," *Diabetes Forecast*, May 2002.

Kate McClare, "Destructive Disease," *Boca Raton News*, November 24, 1999.

Internet Sources

American Diabetes Association, "Diabetes Prevention Program Yields Success." www.diabetes.org.

————, "Pre-Diabetes Affects Millions." www.diabetes.org.

Children with Diabetes, "Andrew." www.childrenwithdiabetes.com.

————, "Injected with Life." www.childrenwithdiabetes.com.

————, "Joshua Halberg." www.childrenwithdiabetes.com.

————, "Kelli's Page." www.childrenwithdiabetes.com.

————, "Norm L. Hefner." www.childrenwithdiabetes.com.

————, "Winning with Diabetes." www.childrenwithdiabetes.com.

CNN.com, "Atkins' Diet: Can We Have Our Turkey and Eat It Too?" *Crossfire*, November 26, 1999. www.cnn.com.

Terri D'Arrigo, "Best-Kept Secret or Simply a Gadget?" *American Diabetes Association*. www.diabetes.org.

Diabetic-Lifestyle.com, "The Diabetes Epidemic." www.diabetic-lifestyle.com

Enchanted Kingdom, "Daily Life with Diabetes." http://members.tripod.com.

Holly Firfer, "Herbal Remedies Unproven as Diabetes Treatments." www.diabetic-help.com.

Kidney Directions, "Diabetes Management." www.kidneydirections.com.

Chris Kuell, "Trips for the Newly Blind Diabetic," *Voice of the Diabetic*, vol. 14, no. 3, Summer 1999, *National Federation of the Blind*. www.nfb.org.

Lifescan.com, "Diabetes Growing Fastest in Asia." www.lifescan. com.

Tom Majeski, "Diabetes Is on Rise Among U.S. Somalis," *Diabetes Newswire*. www.twincities.com.

Rick Mendosa, "Native American Diabetes," *American Diabetes Association*. www.diabetes.org.

National Institute of Diabetes and Digestive and Kidney Disorders, "The Pima Indians Pathfinders for Health." www.niddk. nih.gov.

Christopher D. Saudek, "Progress and Promise of Diabetes Research," *JAMA*. www.jama.ama-assn.org.

Neil M. Scheffler, "One Step Ahead of Amputation," *American Diabetes Association*. www.diabetes.org.

Index

ackee fruit, 60–61

acupuncture, 56–58

African Americans, 20, 81

alcohol, 71

allylpropyl-disulfide, 83–84

alpha-lipoic acid, 50

American Diabetes Association
  camps for diabetic
    children, 76–77
  diet recommended by,
    40–41
  genetic research programs
    of, 86–87
  school problems of
    diabetics reported by, 70
  weight loss recommended
    by, 66

American Dietetic Association,
  81

amputation, 26–27, 72–73

Anderson, James W., 82

antioxidants, 49–50, 83–84

aromatherapy, 56

Asia, 11

Atkins, Robert, 48–49

Australia, 11

autoimmunity, 16–17

beans, 62

Bernstein, Gerald, 64

beta cells, 49
  see also pancreas,
    diagram of

blindness, 23–24, 73–74

blood glucose monitors,
  63–64, 74, 90–91

blood sugar. *See* glucose

blood tests, 31–32

bracelets, 74

B vitamins. *See* antioxidants;
  vitamin B complex

camps, 76–77

carbohydrates, 41–42

cardiac problems, 24–25

Centers for Disease Control
  and Prevention, 10

chelation therapy, 58

Cockram, Clive, 11

dehydroepiandrosterone.
  See DHEA

depression, 67–68

DHEA (dehydroepiandro
  sterone), 50–51

diabetes, 10
  alcohol and, 71
  alternative treatments for,
    45–61
  amputation and, 72–73
  awareness programs for, 13
  blindness and, 73–74
  chronic nature of, 16
  complications of, 22–28
  diagnosis of, 29–33
  diet and, 40–42, 78–81
  education about, 76–77
  epidemic status of, 10–11
  exercise and, 42–44, 78–81
  feet and, 73
  genetics and, 20, 86–89
  immune system and, 16–17
  impact of, on society, 13
  incurability of, 16
  kidneys and, 16
  lack of known cause, 16
  lifestyle and, 78–79
  management of,
    62–67, 68–71
  medications for, 38–40
  modern life and, 78–81
  nicotine and, 72–73
  nutrients and, 81–85
  race and, 20–21
  risk factors for, 19–21
  school environments and,
    68–70
  social situations and, 68
  statistics for, 10–11, 22, 78
  teenagers and, 70–71
  testing for, 31–32
  theories about, 16–17
  treatments for, 89–91
  weight and, 65–67
  see also type I diabetes;
    type II diabetes
Diabetes Educator (journal), 46
diabetes ketoacidosis (DKA),
  27–28
Diabetes Prevention Program
  (DPP), 80–81
diabetic neuropathy,
  25–27, 85–86
diabetic retinopathy, 22–24
diagnosis, 29–33
dialysis, 24
dietary fiber, 82
dietary treatments, 46–49
dieticians, 67
dimethyl sulfoxide (DMSO),
  59
DKA. *See* diabetes ketoacidosis
DMSO. *See* dimethyl sulfoxide
DNA, 87–88
  see also genetics
DPP. *See* Diabetes Prevention
  Program
drinking, 71
drugs, 38–40
Drum, David, 53

equipment, 74
ethnicity, 20–21
exercise, 42–44
eyes, 73–74

family tendency. *See* genetics
fatigue, 30
FDA (Food and Drug
    Administration), 45–46
feet, 25–26, 73
fenugreek, 60
fiber, 82
Food and Drug Administra-
    tion. *See* FDA
free radicals, 49–50

Gaines-Gray, Elizabeth, 79
garlic, 83–84
genes, 87–88
    see also genetics
genetics, 20, 86–89
ginseng, 52–53, 60
glucose
    depression and, 67–68
    eating and, 15
    excess of, 16, 22
    exercise and, 42
    fiber and, 82
    food and, 40–42, 62
    garlic and, 83–84
    glycogen form of, 15
    monitoring of, 62–65
    onions and, 84–85
    overeating and, 65–66
    purpose of, in human body,
        14
    regulation of, 64–65
    storage of, 15
    stress and, 27–28, 53, 62

    tablet form, 74
    yoga and, 55
glucose meters, 90–91
Gluco Watch Biographer, 90–91
glycogen, 71
Guagliani, Diane, 40
gymnema, 51–52

heart attack, 24–25
herbs, 51–53
heredity. *See* genetics
Hispanics, 20, 81, 82
hunger, 30
hypoglycemia, 39–40, 74

immune system, 16–17
infection, 25–27
insulin
    diet and, 41–42
    dosages of, 34–35
    fiber and, 82
    injection of, 33–34
        with "pen," 35-36
        pumps and, 37-38, 90
    overdosage of, 39–40
    pancreas and, 15
    patch for, 89
    pill, 89–90
    role of, in human body, 15
    sources of, 33
    sprayable testing for, 89
    types of, 33–35
islets of Langerhans. *See* pan-
    creas, diagram of

jet injectors, 37
journal keeping, 64–65
Journal of the American Medical Association, 91
juvenile onset diabetes, 17
  see also type I diabetes

ketoacidosis, 70, 71
ketones, 27–28
Khan, Mahmood, 79
kidneys, 16, 24
Kitabchi, Abbas E., 27–28
Knowler, Bill, 80, 88
Koplan, Jeff, 12–13

lanolin, 73
Latinos. *See* Hispanics
Lawrence Review of Natural Products (journal), 84
legs, 25–27
legumes, 82

Mariott, Bernadette, 61
Mayo Clinic, 50, 79
medical bracelets, 74
meditation, 53–54
metaformin, 88
Milchovich, Sue K., 40
mind-body treatments, 53–56
monitors, 63–64, 74, 90–91
National Diabetes Conference, 79
National Institute of Diabetes and Digestive and Kidney Diseases, 64, 80-81

National Institutes of Health
  acupuncture recommended by, 56
  diabetes awareness programs of, 13
  Native American studies of, 80, 87–88
Native Americans, 20–21, 79–81, 82, 87–88
necklaces, 73–74
needles, 35
nervous system, 25–27
nicotine, 72–73
numbness, 25–26

onions, 84–85

pancreas, 15, 78, 81
  diagram of, 14
pills, 38–40
Pima, 79–81, 87–88
prediabetes, 88–89
protein, 42

quercetin, 84–85

race, 20–21
retinopathy, 73–74
Rubin, Alan L., 18–19

Saudek, Christopher, 81, 91
Scheffler, Neil M., 26–27
Scott, Warren A., 42, 44
self-monitoring, 63–67
Shimer, Porter, 42, 64

smoking, 72–73
Somali immigrants, 79
stress, 27–28, 53–54
stroke, 24–25
sugar, 14–16
    see also glucose
supplies, 74

teenagers, 70–71
test strips, 63–64
Thompson, Tommy G., 88–89
Tuomilehto, Jaako, 86
type I diabetes, 17
    glucose levels for, 33
    symptoms of, 29–30
    testing for, 33
type II diabetes, 18

body shape and, 19
glucose levels for, 33
obesity and, 19
symptoms of, 29–30
testing for, 33
weight and, 19

urination, 29–30

vegetarian diets, 47–48
vision, 73–74
vitamin B complex, 85–86

World Health Organization, 56

yoga, 54–55

Picture Credits

Cover Photo: © Mark Clarke/SPL/Photo Researchers, Inc.
© Associated Press/J. Pat Carter, 23, 80, 87
© Associated Press/Michael Dwyer, 76
© Associated Press/Will Kincaid, 12
© Atkins Center/Getty Images, 49
© Ron Chapple/Thinkstock/PictureQuest, 65
© Custom Medical Stock Photo, 26, 31
© Cygus/Getty Images, 91
© Michael P. Gadomski/Photo Researchers, Inc., 63
© Michael Keller/CORBIS, 47
© Library/Photo Researchers, Inc., 11, 18, 36, 54, 66, 69
© Lineworks, Inc., 14, 15, 17, 30
© McIntyre/Photo Researchers, Inc., 37, 50
© Michael Newman/Photo Edit, 74
    PhotoDisc, 34, 39, 43, 50, 55, 57, 72, 83, 84, 86
© Perry Reichanadter, 21
© Kjell B. Sandved/Photo Researchers, Inc., 52, 60
© Steve Zmina, 41

About the Author

Barbara Sheen has been a writer and educator for more than thirty years. She writes in both English and Spanish. Her fiction and nonfiction books have been published in the United States and Europe. She currently lives in Texas with her family where she enjoys weight training, swimming, cooking, and reading. This is her fifth book in Lucent's Diseases and Disorders series.